# Railways of South Wales

Adrian Kenny

Ian Allan

PUBLISHING

**Front cover:** The loco-hauled Rhymney trains started off with Pete Waterman's No 47488 *Davies the Ocean* on Monday 25 September 1995 and continued for more than 11 years, finishing with EWS's No 37410 on Monday 11 December 2006. In between, the service trains were worked variously by '71A Locomotives Ltd' 'Slim Jim' No 33208, No 50031 *Hood* of 'The Fifty Fund', EWS and Res Class 47s, numerous EWS 37s, EWS's No 56114, various Riviera Trains 47s and (for one week only) West Coast Railway Company's No 47854. On rugby days in Cardiff, other companies and classes saw use including, among others, Fragonset's No 31459, DRS's No 37611, Fragonset's No 47703, a couple of EWS 66s and 'Hastings Diesels Limited's DEMU No 1001!

Normally, the stabling of these trains was such that a shot like this would be impossible. However, the previous day was the official opening to passengers of the Vale of Glamorgan line and Nos 37425 and 37411 had been out in top'n'tail mode to celebrate this fact, which, upon their return to Rhymney, led to this unique arrangement.

On Monday 13 June 2005, No 37408 is seen backing into Rhymney station in readiness to form 2V07, the 06:59 to Cardiff. On the left is No 37411 in BR Green, which will form the third train down, 2F06, the 07:39 Rhymney to Cardiff. That leaves No 37425 in Large Logo to form the middle service, 2F05, the 07:17 Rhymney to Cardiff.

**Back cover:** The line between Craven Arms and Llanelli is known as the Central Wales Line and is marketed under the Heart of Wales banner. It is justifiably renowned for its spectacular scenic views, which is why both diesel and steam trains traverse the line several times a year on charters for both enthusiasts and ordinary punters.

The line passes through several tunnels and over two magnificent viaducts at Cynghordy and Knucklas. The latter, complete with castellated turrets, is seen set amongst its surroundings as 1Z38, the 16:45 Llandrindod Wells to Eastleigh service, rumbles over it. Nos 37422 *Cardiff Canton* and 37417 *Richard Trevithick* are hauling 11 well-patronised coaches as Pathfinder Tours' 'The Heart of Wales Explorer' on Saturday 25 August 2007.

**Title page:** As is common with a lot of South Wales coal branches, loaded coal trains can often be seen going both up and down the valley. In this case a train of 22 MEAs had been loaded at Parc Slip the day before and, because no Class 60 was available, the train had to be split into two rakes of 11 MEAs to be taken up to Celtic Energy's site at Cwmbargoed for washing and blending. Here, after discharge, No 66142 rumbles down the Taff Bargoed valley with the first set of 11 empty MEAs in tow forming the 6C26 13:08 SO Cwmbargoed to Margam Knuckle Yard, on Saturday 17 June 2000.

The train is passing the fascinating infrastructure remains of the former Nant Y Ffin No 2 small mine, which is recorded as being officially abandoned on 22 November 1986. The windhouse, rusty drams and a loop of narrow-gauge track to the discharge point can all be seen in this view. If one looks hard enough, in the far distance No 66233 can just be seen reversing down from the pad to the sidings after being unloaded.

# Contents

Preface 3

First published 2010

ISBN 978 0 7110 3477 8

Published by Ian Allan Publishing

an imprint of Ian Allan Publishing Ltd, Hersham, Surrey, KT12 4RG
Printed in England by Ian Allan Printing Ltd, Hersham, Surrey, KT12 4RG

Distributed in the United States of America and Canada by BookMasters Distribution Services

Visit the Ian Allan Publishing website at www.ianallanpublishing.com

# PREFACE

## Introduction

The railways of South Wales have always provided a rich source of fascination and wonderment. Their history is magnificently complicated and undeniably compelling, but I cannot even begin to do it justice in the space available here. Therefore I will leave the reader to delve into the many history books available that cover this topic and will instead just concentrate on the era since privatisation.

## The book

I originally intended this book to cover all of the lines, branch lines, preservation lines, industrial locations, train companies, loco classes, unit classes, sub-classes, liveries, commodities, wagon types, coaching stock and non-coaching stock types that could have been seen in South Wales over the past ten years or so. To do this I started making some lists and found that Wales has seen 11 Train Operating Companies (TOCs), 9 Freight Operating Companies (FOCs), and 31 other main-line operators; some 26 loco classes (59 sub-classes); 14 unit/'Voyager' classes (23 sub-classes); more than 160 liveries; at least 42 distinct types of commodity; and 120 or more different wagon types, not including the many varieties of departmental wagon, guards vans, coaching stock or parcels/ Travelling Post Office (TPO) vehicles!

However, as this book is only 128 pages long, that aim would have been, well, 'difficult'! So I intend, as best I can, to give the broadest representation possible of the quite amazing variety of freight and passenger trains that have been seen in South Wales over the past 13 years.

Bearing in mind that the vast majority of workings occur within a small area of southeast Wales, to help spread the mix of locations I have extended the photographs to include Pilning and Awre, the Welsh connection being that Newport Power Signal Box (PSB) controls the lines to those locations and obviously any traffic on those lines is either destined for, or comes from, Wales. For similar reasons, the book covers the Marches line as far as Craven Arms, where the Heart of Wales line joins.

The photographs in this book have all been taken between April 1998 and September 2009; however, the preface and captions are up to date as far as February 2010. Despite what many may think,

the railways are changing, fast, every month. In the gap between the photographic and written deadlines, South Wales has seen the arrival of the class 70s, Direct Rail Services (DRS) have run their first revenue earning (scrap) trains and, for the first time, both steel slab and Hot Rolled Coil (HRC) have run to Cardiff Docks. Clearly, South Wales has much of interest to offer the enthusiast.

The reader will be taken on a journey starting in the east then heading slowly west, stopping off at most branch lines or valley routes along the way. All photographs were taken with a Mamiya 645 camera using Fuji Provia 100, 100F, 400 or 64T film.

## Passenger services and stations

Improvements to the Welsh passenger network during the privatised era have been on an enormous scale. Since the beginning of 1996:

- Merthyr station was relocated and opened in January 1996.
- Baglan station opened on 2 June 1996, adding a fifth Swanline station to those opened in 1994.
- A third platform was added at Radyr in May 1998.
- Platform 0 at Cardiff Central was opened in August 1999 as part of the station's refurbishment.
- Mountain Ash station was completely replaced by a new facility in January 2001.
- Half-hourly Cardiff to Paddington trains started in May 2001.
- A second platform at Bargoed opened in June 2001.
- Half-hourly services to Aberdare began in December 2003.
- The 'Vale of Glamorgan line' reopened in June 2005 with an hourly service.
- After platform lengthening, four-car units on the Aberdare line began from the June 2005 timetable.
- A 'Standard Pattern Timetable' was introduced in December 2005.
- Shortly after, train frequencies to Bargoed were doubled to every 15 minutes.
- Platform 4 at Newport was opened in August 2007.
- Llanharan station opened in December 2007.
- The Ebbw Vale line, complete with six new stations, reopened to passengers between February and June 2008.
- After platform lengthening, the possibility of operating four-car units on the Maesteg line became available from December 2008.

Left: Even in the times of British Rail (BR), Class 40 visits to South Wales were few and far between, rarely making it further west than the yards at Severn Tunnel Junction. The class's final visit before withdrawal came about in May 1987, when celebrity No 40122 worked a week-long set of Holyhead to Cardiff turns.

Of the 200 English Electric Type 4s built for BR at the Vulcan Foundry Works in Newton-le-Willows between 1958 and 1962, a healthy seven made it into preservation. Of these, only the Class Forty Preservation Society's No 40145 is main-line operational, making a welcome return to the network on 28 October 2002 on a test run, prior to working its first railtour on 30 November.

It has since made several welcome forays into South Wales on a variety of railtours. Here, in BR Blue, it has a load of 11 behind it hauling Pathfinder Tours' 'The Welsh Central Liner II' on Saturday 3 March 2007. The 'II' refers to the fact that this was only the second ever visit of a Class 40 to the Heart of Wales line – the first being by No 40035 *Apapa* on 3 April 1984. This train is the 1Z47 05:44 Crewe to Llandrindod Wells via Cardiff, and it is about to pass under the Wye Bridge.

- During 2007 and 2008 those platforms of only four-car length on the lines between Rhymney, Treherbert and Penarth were lengthened ready to take six-car units in the future (with the sole exception of Gilfach Fargoed 'International').
- A half-hourly train service to Merthyr started in May 2009.

However, balanced against this has been the loss of through services from South Wales to such places as Birmingham International, Brighton, Glasgow, Liverpool, Newcastle, Penzance, Stansted, Waterloo and Weymouth.

As well as all the previous good work in reopening lines to passenger usage, there is still more proposed. On the main line:
- A fourth platform at Severn Tunnel Junction (STJ) opened in January 2010 in conjunction with the remodelling scheme.
- The planned redevelopment of Llanwern Steelworks might see a new station on the upgraded relief lines to serve it. However, this will probably be at the expense of a station at Magor/Undy.
- Two extra platforms at Cardiff Central are proposed.
- In the long term, stations are hoped for at Brackla, St Mellons and Coedkernew.

On the North & West (N&W) route:
- A station is proposed at Caerleon.
- In the long term, stations are proposed at Llantarnam and Sebastopol.
- There are long-term proposals for a half-hourly frequency to Abergavenny, which would have a third turnback platform.

On the Ebbw Vale line:
- Hourly passenger services to Newport are proposed, which will mean a half-hourly service to Ebbw Vale.
- An extension of the line, to Ebbw Vale town centre.
- Reinstatement of passenger services between Aberbeeg and Abertillery.
- Two additional stations at Pye Corner and Cwm.

On the Cardiff Valley lines:
- Six-car units operating on the Treherbert, Rhymney and Penarth lines.
- Two extra platforms at Cardiff Queen Street.
- Half-hourly services to Rhymney.
- Half-hourly services on the Vale of Glamorgan line.

- An increase in the number of trains between Cardiff Queen Street and Cogan Junction from 12 to 16 per hour.
- An additional station at Energlyn.
- Additional turnback platforms at Barry, Pontypridd and Caerphilly.
- If the proposals for RAF St Athan came to fruition, a station at Gileston.

On the Maesteg line:
- The introduction of half-hourly services.

Other schemes include:
- The reinstatement of part of the former Cwm coking-works line, with stations at Talbot Green, Llantrisant, Gwaun Meisgyn and Beddau.
- Reinstatement of passenger services between Aberdare and Hirwaun.

On Saturday 4 May 2002 the Football Association (FA) Cup Final was played in Cardiff's Millennium Stadium, with Arsenal beating Chelsea 2–0. As usual, many extra and strengthened services were run, some of which were loco-hauled and some of which weren't. One of many such trains that day was three-car No 150012 (formed of Nos 150112 and 57206), seen rushing through the site of the former Undy troughs with an unidentified Central Trains service to Cardiff.

- A fifth service on the Heart of Wales line.
- A new branch to Cardiff International Airport.

Research reveals that since 1983 some 5 former freight-only lines have been restored to passenger use and some 39 new stations added to the network, with more set to come.

## Train Operating Companies (TOCs)

Of the original 25 privatised TOCs, five could be found operating in South Wales. These were:

- Great Western Holding's 'Great Western Trains' (GWT).
- Prism Rail's 'South West and Wales' (SW&W).

- Prism Rail's 'Cardiff Railway Company' (CRC).
- Virgin's 'Cross Country' (VXC).
- Prism Rail's 'Central Trains' (CT).

GWT covered InterCity trains from South Wales to Paddington and was awarded to a management buyout, backed by '3i' and 'First Bus', in February 1996. First Bus changed its name to the First Group and bought out GWT in March 1998.

The 'Greater Western' franchise, combining GWT, First Great Western Link (Thames Trains) and Wessex Trains, was won again by the First Group and began in April 2006 for a period of ten years.

SW&W started operations in October 1996, but renamed itself 'Wales and West' (W&W) in December 1997. All of Prism Rail's

A major shake-up of the franchises in 2007 saw the Virgin Cross Country and Central Trains franchises abolished and split between a new Cross Country franchise (won by Arriva), a new London Midland franchise (won by Govia), a new East Midlands Trains franchise (won by Stagecoach) and the existing Virgin West Coast and TransPennine Express franchises.

Thus from November 2007 Arriva Cross Country (AXC) began running not only the single 'Voyager' service in South Wales, but also the Class 170-operated hourly Cardiff to Nottingham trains. The AXC franchise will run until April 2016 with a provision for termination after six years if certain performance criteria are not met. In the predominantly brown and silver colours of AXC, No 170103 is seen rushing through Llandevenny with the 11:45 Cardiff to Nottingham service on Wednesday 9 September 2009.

In the background is the 200-yard Bishton flyover. This was opened on 17 April 1961 in order to give trains from the new Spencer (now Llanwern) Steelworks uninterrupted access to the up yard at Severn Tunnel Junction without the need to cross the up and down main lines on the level. Whether it is needed today is perhaps open for debate, but in 2010 it remains as a testament to previous busier times.

franchises were sold to the National Express Group in October 2000. In September 2001 the Strategic Rail Authority (SRA) split W&W into two temporary franchises, 'Wales and Borders' & 'Wessex Trains', as a prelude to the combining of all Welsh services under one roof. It was the Arriva Group that won this 15-year franchise in December 2003.

The CRC franchise began in October 1996 for a period of 7½ years. However, it was merged into the new W&B franchise after less than five years.

VXC began operations in January 1997 serving Wales just once a day. The franchise was meant to finish in March 2012 but was 'reorganised' well before that.

The CT franchise began in March 1997 and consisted of services from both Cardiff and Hereford to various destinations by way of Birmingham. A major shake-up of the franchises in 2007 saw the VXC and CT operations abolished and split between various other franchises. The new 'Cross Country' franchise, won by Arriva, began running in November of that year.

Thus in 2010, only three TOCs, First Great Western, Arriva Trains Wales and Arriva Cross Country, could be found operating passenger trains in South Wales.

## Freight

It is important to remember that the railways are merely there to provide a service to their various customers. Thus the freight railways of South Wales have grown and shrunk in relation to the industries they have served. Although space makes it impossible to list here every individual flow that has been won or lost in the past decade, it is possible to have a more general look at things.

Some lines or sidings are mothballed when the site they serve finishes production, but reopen again years later when a new facility is developed. Examples of this include the lines to Uskmouth, Cwmbargoed and Gwaun Cae Gurwen (GCG).

Some lines, at the time of writing, remain in a mothballed state. A few examples include the branches to Port Talbot Grange, Port Talbot Docks and Swansea Docks.

Other terminals have apparently closed, but the traffic has in fact continued by rail, albeit from a different loading point. Examples of this include the relocation of the intermodal terminal from Pengam to Wentloog, and stone, once loaded at Hereford, which is now loaded at Moreton on Lugg.

Further sites have been reopened for specific one-off contracts.

Two such examples include Waterston, for stone traffic, and Carmarthen sidings, for pipe traffic.

Some terminals only operate on an as-required basis. Examples include Orb Steelworks for export steel coil and Haverfordwest for Ministry of Defence (MoD) traffic.

There have been a few trials that unfortunately have not led to any further rail traffic. Examples include fertiliser to Haverfordwest, chipped tyres to Aberthaw Cement Works and limestone to Llantrisant yard.

There are also examples of freight appearing in South Wales that is neither destined for nor originates from there. Examples have included china clay from Cornwall to Cliffe Vale, Mossend or Irvine; coal from Portbury and Avonmouth to Rugeley or Fiddlers Ferry; and steel coil from Goole or Immingham to Swindon.

There have inevitably been numerous terminal and line closures during the past ten years. Examples include Baglan Bay, Canton Tablogix and Ebbw Vale, among numerous others.

Equally, however, since privatisation there have been a number of success stories. At Newport Docks there has been a new rail-connected 'No 7' shed for steel-coil traffic, a new bulk-coal terminal, and a new line to SIMS Metals. A new siding to European Metal Recycling (EMR) in Cardiff Docks opened in April 2002; a new slab-loading terminal known as Port Talbot Field opened in June 2005; a new scrap siding was opened in Barry Docks in April 2008; and a new service to Bird Port began in May 2009.

At the time of writing (February 2010) I found that there were 30 terminals or sidings in use for railfreight traffic. Some of these locations receive or dispatch more than one type of product; for instance, the Tower pad can load out both coal and stone, and Wentloog handles both intermodal and MoD traffic, but both locations have only been counted once. Other areas have several loading or unloading points within their boundary. For instance, Newport Docks can be said to have six distinct areas where rail traffic can either be received or dispatched and these have been counted separately.

I have defined a mothballed terminal or line as one that has not been (officially) shut and could, theoretically at least, come back on stream at any point in the near future. Using this basis, I reckoned that 23 such places currently exist in South Wales.

Finally, there are what I consider to be 41 terminals that are either out of use or have been permanently closed during the time frame of this book with no, or very little, hope of being reactivated.

**Right:** As part of a shuffle of units in May 2001, three of Cardiff Railway Company's Class 143s were transferred to Wales & West, being replaced by five of Newton Heath's 142s in GMPTE (Greater Manchester Passenger Transport Executive) livery. At the time, the extra two units allowed the number of loco-hauled Rhymney trains to be reduced from two to one.

Having arrived less than a month earlier, GMPTE-liveried No 142006 finds itself partnered with Valley Lines-liveried No 143605 *Crimestoppers* on an unidentified service from Barry Island, approaching Eastbrook on Sunday 10 June 2001.

Right: Uskmouth 'B' Power Station was rail-served with coal right from its opening in 1961. The 1984–85 miners' strike saw rail deliveries stop, and from that date the power station was served by road until its closure in 1995. It was bought by Allied Energy Systems (AES) in January 1998, which controversially renamed it Fifoots. Rail deliveries recommenced on 19 March 2000, but stopped a little under two years later when the owning company went into receivership. The station was then bought by Carron Energy, which thankfully renamed it back to Uskmouth. Rail deliveries started again from 17 August 2004 and have continued on and off since that time.

Part of the condition of the original reopening was that all deliveries were to be by rail. Under AES's ownership, this included the lime that was sourced from Hindlow in the Peak District and delivered by 'Enterprise'. The first delivery was on 18 August 2000, using a small fleet of former Rugby Cement wagons, which English Welsh & Scottish (EWS) Railways had bought, refurbished, painted into corporate colours and recoded CSA. Deliveries were four wagons at a time from a pool of eight, on an as-required basis. With a friendly wave from the travelling shunter, No 56038 is recorded working the 6F06 10:31 'Q' Alexandra Dock Junction (ADJ) to Fifoots on Friday 14 December 2001, seen rumbling down the start of the branch to the power station.

## Freight Operating Companies (FOCs)

There are seven FOCs that have operated their own services in South Wales since 1996. These are:

- Deutsche Bahn Schenker (DBS) West, formerly EWS
- Freightliner
- Mendip Rail
- GBRf
- Cotswold Rail/Advenza Freight
- Colas Rail
- Direct Rail Services (DRS)

The locos of two other FOCs have also been seen in the area for various reasons, but have not worked their own company trains:

- Fastline
- National Power

Unfortunately, the list of workings that they have undertaken, or have been seen on, is too long to be incorporated into this Preface, but I have done my best to scatter them throughout the various captions.

There have also been some 31(!) other main-line operators seen in South Wales, including the likes of the Diesel Traction Group, Fragonset, Ian Riley and Riviera Trains.

## Infrastructure

Often forgotten in the larger picture is the railway infrastructure. Again, South Wales has its fair share of variation. The South Wales main line has four tracks between STJ and Cardiff, but is just a single line between Cockett and Duffryn. There are numerous viaducts and several tunnels, including the longest tunnel on the British network, the 4-mile 628-yard Severn Tunnel.

The infrastructure has seen numerous changes over the past 13 years. As well as numerous smaller rationalisations (some in association with the South Wales resignalling scheme), some of the bigger improvement schemes have been:

- The creation of a much simplified and faster layout at Radyr in May 1998.
- A new loop at Mountain Ash in January 2001.
- The refurbishment of the Ebbw Vale line, starting in 2006.
- A revised and simpler layout at the west end of Newport station during August 2007.
- An altered layout at Abercynon in May 2008, so that it became a junction station once more.
- The long-talked-about passing loop at Merthyr Vale was built at the same time.
- The creation of a faster layout at STJ, undertaken over the Christmas 2009 and New Year 2010 break.

Keen not to rest on its laurels, the Welsh Assembly Government and Network Rail have several other infrastructure schemes in various stages of development. On the main line, these include:

- Speed improvements to the relief lines between Severn Tunnel Junction and Cardiff.
- Reinstatement of the double lead to Ebbw Vale at Gaer Junction, controversially removed in August 2005.
- An improved Chepstow turnback capability.

On the N&W route these include:

- A long-term plan for an additional turnback facility at Abergavenny.
- An increase in line speeds.

On the Ebbw Vale line these include:

- An extension of the line north to Ebbw Vale town.
- Additional track to allow half-hourly services.
- The reinstatement of the former Ebbw Fach valley line as far as Abertillery.

On the Valley Lines:

- A new loop at Tir-Phil or extension of the double track from Bargoed.
- Extra tracks at Cardiff Queen Street.
- Additional turnback facilities at Barry, Pontypridd and Caerphilly.
- Double-tracking the Treforest curve through Canton.
- Speed improvements on the City line.

Other schemes include:

- A passenger loop on the Maesteg line.
- The reinstatement of 5 miles of double track from Cockett to Duffryn, including the complete renewal of Loughor Viaduct.
- The reinstatement of the line for passengers between Pontyclun and Beddau.
- A new branch from Porthkerry into Cardiff Airport.
- Network Rail's NSIP (National Station Improvement) scheme.

The Department for Transport announced on 23 July 2009 that immediate work would begin on a £1billion scheme to electrify the South Wales main line. The section from London (Airport Junction) to Bristol (via both Badminton and Chippenham), together with 'stubs' to Oxford and Newbury, would be complete by 2016, and the line to Swansea by 2017. Certainly, interesting times lie ahead.

## Signalling

South Wales has much variety signalling-wise, with semaphores and two-, three- or four-aspect Multiple Aspect Signalling (MAS) controlled both by track circuits and axle counters. The former lamps are being replaced by new Light Emitting Diode (LED) signals.

There are eight different types of signalling system used in South Wales:

- Track Circuit Block (TCB)
- Absolute Block (AB), sometimes in conjunction with Intermediate Block (IB) signals
- No Signalman Token (NST)
- No Signalman Token Remote (NSTR)

Far right: Class 58s were never common in South Wales, only appearing in their dying years on fly ash, engineer's services, stone trains and railtours, together with a few other 'one-off' trips. The class's first and, unsurprisingly, only appearance at Tondu was on the 'Worksop Depot Class 58 Farewell Tour' on Saturday 1 July 2000.

The train of 13 coaches had begun the day as the 1Z58 06:22 Worksop to Cardiff behind Nos 58037 *Worksop Depot* and 58024. Upon reaching Cardiff the train continued as the 1Z90 11:40 Cardiff to Cardiff via Barry and Swansea Burrows sidings, where No 60070 took the train via the Ogmore Vale line to Tondu. This meant that the 58s were leading again for the return, and they are pictured here leaving Tondu, with the 60 out of sight on the rear. At Cardiff the 60 was detached and the 58s returned the train to Worksop.

**Right:** For a while in 1999 and 2000, two Class 143s, Nos 143611 and 143613, were painted up in a rather garish 'Valley Fun Days' livery. The latter of these two unfortunate units is seen here slowing for the stop at Pengam station with the 17:15 Rhymney to Cardiff service on Saturday 27 May 2000.

Even more unfortunate for No 143613 was 18 October 2004, when a mechanical failure meant that it suffered a serious fire near Nailsea & Backwell while working the 2W63 20:06 Bristol Temple Meads to Weston-super-Mare service with No 143621. One of the coaches was completely gutted and the other was so badly damaged that the unit was eventually withdrawn. Remarkably, No 143621 escaped relatively unscathed.

No 143613 was actually the second unit to catch fire, as No 143615 had self-immolated in mid-2004 and was also subsequently withdrawn. Both units spent some time at Crewe before being returned to Canton and broken up in mid 2006. Jokes along the lines of 2 down, 23 to go were commonplace at the time.

- One Train Working (OT)
- One Train Working with Staff (OT(S))
- Train Staff and Ticket (TST)
- C2 lines

The number of signal boxes has been steadily reducing over the years. However, there have also been several positive developments:
- Additional signalling between Cardiff Central and Queen Street.
- A new mini-panel installed at Abercynon to control the resignalled Cynon Valley line, in conjunction with the reopening of the line to passenger trains.
- Additional signalling along the Vale of Glamorgan controlled by a new mini-panel in Aberthaw signal box, again in association with reintroduced passenger trains.
- Additional signalling between Ystrad Mynach and Bargoed.
- New signalling on the Ebbw Vale line, after the introduction of passenger trains to that line.
- Most recently, Abercynon signal box was replaced with a panel box.

There are currently (February 2010) 25 operational signal boxes in South Wales:

- Three Power Signal Boxes
- Five panel-only boxes
- Ten lever-only boxes
- Five boxes that have both levers and a mini-panel
- One industrial-user box
- One box on a preservation line

In addition, there are:

- Three level-crossing-only boxes
- One former box used as a ground frame
- One box used as a combined level crossing and ground frame
- Three other former signal boxes extant but privately owned

There is considerable variety in signal-box duties. At one end of the scale, Bishton crossing box has just a level crossing to control, but interestingly has the only wheel-operated crossing in the whole of Wales. In the middle, Clarbeston Road box has both levers and a mini-panel to operate NST to Fishguard, AB to Whitland (with an IB signal in between) and TCB to Milford Haven. At the top end of the scale are the three PSBs, which were all built in the 1960s and, at nearly 40 years old, were/are in need of replacement. That scheme is being undertaken in four parts:

- Part One, the Port Talbot Signalling Renewal (PTSR) scheme from Baglan to Llantrisant, was completed between July 2005 and April 2007.
- As this book was being written, Part Two, the Newport Area Signalling Renewal (NASR), was being undertaken. This scheme has been split into four phases:
  - Phase 1 began in 2008 and covers the line between Patchway and East Usk. It was completed in January 2010, with control of the area being the first to be transferred to the new South Wales Control Centre (SWCC), situated on the site of the former Canton Isis Link depot.
  - Phase 2 covers the line between Maindee West and the fringe with Cardiff at Marshfield, and is due for completion in October 2010.
  - Phase 3 covers works between Caldicot and Awre enabling Newport PSB to close.

- Phase 4 follows the Cardiff Area Signalling Renewal (CASR), when the fringe boxes at Park junction and Little Mill will be abolished and transferred to the SWCC.
- The CASR between Marshfield and Llantrisant will see Cardiff panel box demolished to make way for a proposed new platform.
- Port Talbot's PSB control area will then be migrated to the SWCC.
- There are also plans to install the long-needed Intermediate Block signals on the up line between Abergavenny and Pontrilas.

In the long term, the introduction of ERTMS (the European Rail Traffic Management System) has been mooted; this is an 'in cab' signalling system, set to be trialled on the Cambrian route over the next few years.

## Locos and units

South Wales has seen all available classes of diesel locomotive appear on the main line over the past 13 years, covering everything from Class 08s to Class 67s. A photograph of each type (but not each sub-type) is contained within this book. Even a Class 73 electro-diesel showed up on a working in February 2006, and both Class 86s and 87s have also been seen, albeit by road for scrap, rather than by rail. Freightliners class 70s started arriving in Britain from November 2009 and set to come in the future is the Super Express Train.

There have been 11 types of second-generation Diesel Multiple Units (DMUs) seen in South Wales over the same period, ranging from Class 142s to Class 221s, and again a sample of each type (except one, the Class 159) can be found in this book. Even two types of first-generation DMUs will be found among these pages.

South Wales is, of course, rich in industrial heritage. Despite numerous rationalisations, there have been some 15 locations in the past 13 years or so that have employed their own, or hired in, industrial shunters to work internal sidings or systems. In alphabetical order, these are:

- Allied Steel & Wire/Celsa and Cardiff Docks
- Baglan Bay chemical works
- Caerwent Training Area
- Ebbw Vale Steelworks
- Ford at Bridgend
- Llandarcy Refinery

The 182 Class 158s were built by British Rail Engineering Limited (BREL) at Derby between 1989 and 1992, and were soon introduced to South Wales to cascade the less suitable Class 155 'Sprinters' and 156 'Super Sprinters' to other, shorter-distance, duties. Despite being outwardly similar, they came in a number of different forms, being of two-car and three-car varieties (Nos 158798-158814), and powered by 350hp Cummins engines (Nos 158701-158814 and 158901-158910), 350hp Perkins engines (Nos 158815-158862) and 400hp Cummins engines (Nos 158863-158872), the third variety being specifically intended for use on the steeply graded Marches line.

Since that time they have been re-formed, de-formed, re-painted, re-vinyled, re-branded and even re-classified, but have visited most of the South Wales branch lines and byways with the exception of only a few of the Cardiff Valley lines, for which they are not passed.

No 158825 is seen at the 'classic' location of St Ishmael, working the 13:23 Milford Haven to Manchester Piccadilly service on Saturday 28 June 2003. Another unidentified 158 is in the distance heading north with a Penzance to Pembroke Dock train.

The Ginsters livery was introduced (on No 158841) on 17 January 2003 and lasted until near the end of 2006. While not the worst advertising livery in the world, the 'Flying Pasties', as these units became known, certainly raised a few eyebrows when first introduced.

- The 'Pontypool and Blaenavon Railway', which operates between Furnace Sidings and Whistle Inn. An extension to Blaenavon High Level is scheduled to open in 2010 and further extensions are planned to Big Pit, Wainfelin and Brynmawr.
- The 'Butetown Historic Railway Society', formed in 1979, which had a short section of line at Bute Road station. The society moved to Barry in 1996 and began operations as the 'Vale of Glamorgan Railway' (VoGR), later marketed as the 'Barry Island Railway'. In November 2008 the VoGR was replaced by 'Cambrian Transport Limited' as operators of the railway. Today the line runs from Barry Plymouth Road to two sites at Gladstone Bridge and Barry Waterfront. Extensions are planned to Barry Docks and maybe Barry Pier.
- Finally, the highly successful 'Gwili Railway' runs between Bronwydd Arms and Danycoed. An extension to Abergwili Junction is ongoing, which will hopefully be followed by one to Llanpumsaint.

In contrast to Mid and North Wales, the south of the country has a relative dearth of narrow-gauge railways.

- The 1ft 11¾in 'Brecon Mountain Railway' operates between Pant and Pontsticill via the Dolygaer run-round loop. An extension to Torpantau has been laid but not yet opened.
- The 2-mile-long, 2-foot-gauge 'Teifi Valley Railway' lies just east of Newcastle Emlyn and runs between Henllan and Llandyfriog (Riverside). The latest passenger extension to the actual site of the former Henllan station opened as recently as July 2009.
- There are also narrow-gauge railways at Margam Country Park, Pembrey Country Park and Oakwood amusement park, but these are not built on former railway lines.
- Further narrow-gauge railways lie unseen at the Castlemartin firing ranges, and there is an extensive 2ft 6in system within the former Trecwn Royal Navy Armaments Depot (RNAD).

- Llanwern Steelworks
- Machen Quarry
- Onllwyn Disposal Point (DP)
- Orb Steelworks
- Port Talbot Steelworks
- Robeston Oil Refinery
- Swansea Marcroft
- Trostre Tinplating Works
- Uskmouth Power Station (PS)

## Preservation and other lines

A large number of the former railway lines in South Wales have, unsurprisingly, been converted into roads. Several more have become cycle paths or scenic walking trails. However, some old lines have been preserved and at the start of 2009, these included:

Three other preservation groups, in the embryonic stages, are worthy of mention. One wishes them much success in the future:

- The 'Amman Valley Railway Society', formed in 1992, has ambitious plans to run passenger trains between Pantyffynnon and Abernant. The reactivation of the GCG line for coal traffic means that only slow (but steady) progress has been made.
- The 'Bridgend Valleys Railway Society' was formed in 1998 to preserve the line between Tondu and Pontycymmer. In March 2006 it changed its name to the 'Garw Valley Railway Company',

and in February 2009 gave the displaced VoGR company a home for its activities. It is hoped that shuttles between Pontycymmer to Pant-y-gog can start running in the near future, and an extension to Llangeinor is eventually planned.

- The 'Llanelli and Mynydd Mawr Railway' was formed in April 1999 and is based at the former Cynheidre Colliery. It initially plans to operate a mile of line northwards from Cynheidre as well as a future industrial and railway heritage museum.

Unfortunately there have also been two preservation casualties:

- The 'Caerphilly Railway Society' finished in 1996. It never had a real running line and most of the stock that was there ended up on the Gwili Railway.
- The second was the 'Swansea Vale Railway'. Unfortunately, owing to a combination of vandalism, increasing land value and lack of passengers, Swansea Council declined to renew its lease in September 2007.

One other group was formed, but because the railway it was going to operate has been reinstated for further use, the plans fell through. This was the 'Vale of Neath Railway Society' at Tonna, which finished when the line to Cwmgwrach reopened in 1994. Other projects have been proposed but have, for various reasons, fallen by the wayside, including at least three schemes in the picturesque Wye Valley.

## Finally

This is, in essence, meant to be a quality photographic book. However, hopefully the reader will also enjoy the detailed information given in this Preface and the captions. It has taken many long hours of research, reading and cross-referencing, but I think (I hope) it has been worth it in the end! The accuracy of the information is something on which I have placed a great deal of emphasis. Therefore, if anyone finds anything, anywhere (at all!) that is incorrect, I would be most pleased to hear from them.

So, all that remains is the 'thank you' part of the book. A sincere thanks must first go to the various gen men for their invaluable information posted to the gen groups, without which many workings would go unrecorded. This also applies to the Freightmaster forum and its various contributors, who have provided a source of invaluable information and discussion. Special mention here needs to be made of 'Slugmaster' for his absolutely invaluable lists. A multitude of thanks are also due to the dozens of other friends and railwaymen who have kindly helped out over the years.

Then there are the various companies that have allowed me access to their works for the industrial photos. In these days of over-zealous lawyers and rigorous health and safety standards, it is far easier for companies to ignore or exclude individuals from their sites than go to the trouble of sanctioning a visit to record these items of valuable interest. It is therefore with a profound sense of gratitude that I am indebted to Len Walsh and Stuart Wilkie at Trostre, and Paul Tremayne at Newport Docks, for allowing me permission to not only visit their sites, but also to publish a photo from that place.

My gratitude also extends in no small way to Ian Allan for their faith in allowing me to compile a book on just a small part of the country. I hope that you, the reader, will find it as fascinating as I do and enjoy looking at and reading this book as much as I have enjoyed preparing it.

**Main line and branches east of Newport**

Cotswold Rail began operations in 2001 as a spot hire company, first for shunters and then for main-line locomotives. The company's locos started running in South Wales in December 2002, being hired in by Freightliner to cover for traction shortages. Cotswold then gained a freight operator's licence in 2004 and purchased the Advenza company in 2005. As Advenza, the company's duties in South Wales have seen it collecting locos and undertaking wagon moves. However, starting on Wednesday 5 March 2008 it began a regular flow of scrap from Stockton to Tidal and then undertook several trial flows to the same place from Beeston, Barry, Tyne Dock, Queens Head, Hitchin and Shipley.

Following this, from October 2008 until its demise in October 2009, the company settled down to running regular trains to Tidal from just Shipley and Stockton. With a mix of 14 KEA/JNA and JRAs in tow, No 57006 and the 6V95 10:22 Stockton to Tidal are seen at Purton rolling alongside the River Severn on Tuesday 23 June 2009.

Right: The South Wales Railway (SWR) Company was incorporated on 4 August 1845 to build a line between Chepstow (West) and Swansea. It was completed in less than five years, an impressive feat of engineering even by today's standards, and the first train ran between the two points on 18 June 1850. The Act allowing the SWR to connect with the Great Western Railway (GWR) was granted on 27 July 1846 and the line from Grange Court Junction to Chepstow (East) opened on 19 September 1851. However, it took a little longer to complete the line between Chepstow east and west as a bridge was required to span the River Wye, which divided the two stations.

The tubular suspension bridge, designed by I. K. Brunel, wasn't opened to traffic until 19 July 1852, being doubled on 18 April 1853. It was this bridge's design that Brunel later used in a much larger form to span the River Tamar at Saltash. Brunel's bridge was replaced in 1962 by the below-deck truss version pictured in the background of this photograph. With a healthy throng of travellers waiting to board, No 156416 calls at Chepstow with the 11:55 Nottingham to Cardiff service on Sunday 30 April 2000.

The Class 170s were introduced by Central Trains to South Wales from the summer 2000 timetable. They were initially intermixed with the company's other units on that route until they displaced first the 156s and later the 158s altogether.

An unidentified Class 170 drifts south through Tidenham on Monday 16 June 2008 with the 08:00 Nottingham to Cardiff service. The ever-changing role of these units within the Train Operating Companies is highlighted by the fact that this 170 carries the former 'Midland Mainline' scheme of teal, grey and tangerine, with 'Central Trains' brandings, even though its operator is now Arriva Cross Country. AXC had absorbed the Cardiff to Nottingham workings as part of its franchise when the Central Trains Train Operating Company (TOC) was formerly disbanded in November 2007.

**Right:** The pleasant evening of Tuesday 24 June 2003 sees doyen of the class, No 60001 *The Railway Observer*, passing under the cable-stayed Wye Bridge with three FCA twins carrying empty lime boxes and 18 loaded BZA/BLAs of hot rolled coil in tow as the 6E30 17:38 FX Margam to Hartlepool. The Severn Suspension Bridge is in the background.

Upon reaching Tees Yard, the FCAs and 'Railfreight Services' boxes will be detached and go forward to Thrislington for loading with dolomite. Starting in 2000, this traffic replaced the former flow of lime from Hardendale, which used a fleet of CBA hoppers and latterly JIA polybulks. The Class 60 will run round and continue to Corus's Hartlepool Works where the coil will be made into pipes for any number of industrial applications.

Since March 2009 Hardendale is once again being used a source of lime, intermixed with Thrislington as required.

**Above:** The growing success of urban services in South Wales can be traced back to 1983 when Tom Clift gave the go-ahead for the opening of Cathays station on the line between Cardiff Queen Street and Radyr. The other 38 stations and five former freight-only lines that have been added to the South Wales passenger network since that time have required additional Class 142s from Manchester and further 150/2s from Anglia, Central Trains, Scot Rail and Wessex to cope with a massive increase in both frequency and size of train.

No 150260 is the subject of this illustration and was one of 12 Scot Rail 150s (Nos 150208/250/252/256/258-260/262/264/283-285) to arrive in May 2005 to strengthen Arriva Trains Wales (ATW) services. It is seen here running through Thornwell after leaving Chepstow with the 16:48 Gloucester to Milford Haven service on Sunday 10 April 2005.

Between 2003 and 2005 vast amounts of redundant Electric Multiple Units (EMUs) were taken from the South East of England to Immingham, Caerwent or Newport Docks for scrapping. The first train to the last-named location ran on Thursday 10 June 2004, using No 66001 to haul Nos 3426, 3427 and 3558 as the 5Z21 15:10 from Shoeburyness with, unlike Caerwent, all subsequent trains running from that location. That train also had the dual honour of being the first service over the newly laid branch to SIMS Metals on the north side of the south dock.

These scrap trains provided the first regular GBRf timetabled services into Wales, with that company taking over from EWS from Wednesday 28 July 2004. Here, uniquely liveried and Medite-branded, No 66709 *Joseph Arnold Davies* and three redundant units, No 312713, 4VEP No 3563 and No 312702, forms the 5Z91 10:40 Shoeburyness to Newport Docks on Wednesday 8 September 2004. After a total 52 movements (all but seven of which were hauled by GBRf), the final scrap EMU train to the docks ran on Monday 27 March 2006.

At 4 miles 628 yards long, the Severn Tunnel is the longest tunnel on the British rail network today. There are two well-known safety protocols associated with the operating of the tunnel. The first is that a train has to clear the exit of the tunnel before the next one can follow it in. The second is that, while a passenger train is in the tunnel, no 'dangerous' goods are allowed to pass it running in the opposite direction. Both these measures mean that the Newport signalmen have to be very 'on the ball' when it comes to regulating trains over this section of line.

No 57003 *Freightliner Evolution* is seen leaving the Up Tunnel Loop and will now enjoy a clear run all the way to Pilning with the 4O51 10:08 Wentloog to Southampton Maritime train formed of 11 FSAs, FTAs and a single KFA. Heading in the opposite direction is No 150251 in the now obsolete Wessex Trains livery, forming a service to Cardiff. The date is Friday 23 April 2004.

Under 'Operation Princess', launched at Birmingham New Street on 30 September 2002, Virgin Cross Country (VXC) increased the number of trains in South Wales from one per day (to Swansea) to seven per day (six to Cardiff and one to Swansea). As part of this increased frequency, Virgin made the Swansea train and one of the Cardiff trains a direct northeast to southwest service via Chepstow, bringing long-distance cross-country trains to this route for the first time since the early 1990s. Sadly the much publicised problems with 'Operation Princess' led to a severe reduction in services to Wales less than a year later, reducing to two trains a day. A short time later they were further reduced to just the current one train a day, and that only to Cardiff instead of Swansea.

'Voyagers' can still be seen along the Chepstow route when engineering work on the Charfield line necessitates diversions via a reversal at STJ or Newport. On Saturday 1 February 2003 No 221136 has just taken the line towards Chepstow with an unidentified northbound service. In the background is the Severn Tunnel Junction Emergency Train with No 09017 *Leo* in charge.

Steam excursions remain an ever-popular feature of the railways today. They operate almost every weekend and often during the week, reaching all corners of the country from Penzance to Thurso. On Saturday 15 September 2007 Past Time Rail took Princess Royal Class Locomotive Trust's (PRCLT's) No 6201 *Princess Elizabeth* on a trip up and down the Marches. EWS's No 67012 brought ten coaches down from Birmingham New Street to Bristol, where No 6201 and its support coach took over for the run to Shrewsbury via Abergavenny.

The return of 'The Welsh Marches Express' ran as a 1Z53 16:03 Shrewsbury to Bristol Temple Meads service and, after a water stop at Magor, is seen accelerating through Severn Tunnel Junction, in the dying evening sunshine.

**Above:** The Class 180 'Adelantes' were introduced on First Great Western (FGW) services from 2001 onwards in order to meet franchise commitments to run half-hourly trains to Cardiff. Despite being thought of as internally superior to 'Voyagers', their mechanical reputation was somewhat worse and, despite efforts, FGW slowly dispensed with the majority of the fleet, replacing them with High Speed Trains (HSTs). Therefore, from the December 2007 timetable change only three units were being run on FGW services, mainly in peak hours along the Cotswold line, but occasionally escaping to Cardiff and other places as well.

The Class 180s bowed out of service with FGW on Friday 27 March 2009 and, although the situation was still fluid at the time of writing, the 14 units were fully employed again variously with Hull Trains, Northern Rail, National Express East Coast and Grand Central.

When rumours of the impending demise of the class with FGW had already started, No 180104 finds itself approaching Severn Tunnel Junction on Monday 3 April 2006 with the 09:55 Cardiff to Paddington service.

**Right:** During the summer of 2004, Wessex Trains were hiring in top'n'tail Class 31s to run strengthened Weymouth trains every weekday, and Fridays-only trains to Brighton. In order to promote the Weymouth services, Fragonset Merlin Rail (FMR) painted No 31601 and five coaches into a garish livery of bright pink.

Its first ever run into Wales in this guise was on Sunday 30 May 2004 for the Division 2 promotion play-off finals, which saw Bristol City lose to Brighton & Hove Albion by a goal to nil. Under deeply threatening skies, No 31601 *Bletchley Park 'Station X'* is top'n'tailing No 31452 *Minotaur* past the site of the former Severn Tunnel Junction up reception sidings on the 5Z73 18:53 Bristol Temple Meads to Cardiff Central service. No 31601 was renamed *The Mayor of Casterbridge* at Bristol Temple Meads on 18 October 2004 and, after FMR's collapse, was sold to Mainline Rail in March 2007. At the beginning of 2009 it was still in pink livery, albeit de-branded, owned by British American Rail Services (BARS) and re-renamed *Gauge 'O' Guild 1956–2006*. BARS repainted 31601 into a deep green in December 2009 and, now de-named, it can be found running around the country on various Serco workings.

Although steel-trains in Wales are dominated by Tata's massive plants at Port Talbot and Llanwern, and to a lesser extent Celsa's plant at Cardiff, in mid 2008 there were still a few other steel-trains that could be observed in South Wales. One was imported steel through Goole Docks and Immingham to Swindon, running via ADJ. The other was steel in the form of beams, girders, channels, angles and Z-sections to Clugston Distribution's terminal, built on the site of the former Bristol East Depot engineer's sidings. The traffic was run to ADJ from Lackenby via 6V49 and from Scunthorpe to ADJ via 6V19, where it was combined to form a 6C01 09:15 ADJ to Bristol East Depot Terminal. The first

train of seven BEAs arrived at Bristol on Monday 4 April 2005 behind No 60083.

On Thursday 12 May 2005 6C01 has No 66199 in charge of 13 loaded BDAs and BEAs, interspersed with eight RRA runner wagons, captured strolling through Undy. Unfortunately, owing to the recession the last train to the site ran on Wednesday 22 October 2008 behind No 60014.

One has to consider the irony of coil to Swindon and finished steel to Bristol being railed from the North East passing within arm's reach of two Welsh plants capable of producing just these products.

InterCity cross-country loco-hauled trains into Wales ceased many years ago, being replaced by HSTs. The only occasions when they have been seen in recent years has been when diversions were necessary away from their normal route through Charfield, or on rare (very rare) HST substitutions. On this occasion, however, power lines had blown down across the line at Winterbourne, necessitating emergency unplanned diversions via Chepstow and a run-round at Newport. Thus No 47853 *Rail Express*, in its celebration XP64 livery, and seven coaches run through Llandevenny with the 1V45 09:13 EWD (every weekday) Liverpool Lime Street to Plymouth service on Saturday 9 March 2002. In the end this train terminated at Exeter St David's some 5 hours and 40 minutes late!

Within just a few months of this photograph being taken No 47853 had been released by Virgin Trains back to Porterbrook, which then sold it on 23 October 2002, together with No 47839, to Riviera Trains, to replace the latter's No 47705, which had been used as No 57303 in the Class 57 conversion programme.

## Newport area: main line, valleys and branches

Newport has, for many years, seen trips run between Llanwern Steelworks, East Usk Yard, Orb Steelworks, Maindee's engineer's sidings, ADJ yard and Newport Docks. This has given the highly unusual and probably unique sight of Class 08s or Class 09s regularly trundling up and down a busy four-track main line.

Class 37s, 60s and 66s have all substituted to cover for motive power shortages and in line with

Deutsche Bahn Schenker (DBS) policy, the sight of little 0-6-0 shunters bobbing their way between the various terminals had all but ceased to be a part of the Newport railway scene in 2009.

One of the pilots' more unusual duties came about on Saturday 28 March 2009, when No 08567 was used on Pathfinder Tours' 'Cwm and Gone' railtour, which had earlier covered the Ogmore Valley Extension to Tondu, the Vale of Glamorgan line and Machen. No 60024 is leading 12 coaches down to the final destination of the day, Uskmouth, as the 1Z60 15:15 from Machen. No 08567 is dead on the rear, ready to later return the train to Newport station.

First Great Western's Nos 43139 and 43026 *City of Westminster* wind themselves over the crossovers on the approach to Newport station with the 1B20 10:00 Paddington to Swansea service on Saturday 30 December 2000.

The train is atop the 215-yard Newport Viaduct. The original two-track, broad-gauge viaduct was just approaching completion when, at 06:00 on 31 May 1848, a hot rivet set fire to adjoining kyanised timbers and almost the entire structure burned down. The reconstruction delayed the opening of the South Wales main line by two years. The widening of the viaduct to accommodate four tracks and the replacement of the centre bowstring arches started in 1913, but it was not until 29 May 1927 that all four lines finally came into use, removing a massive bottleneck in the Newport area.

Behind the HST lies Maindee West Junction where the North & West route to Hereford and Crewe diverges. We will take a trip up that line next.

**Left:** In the 1990s freightliner services in Wales were based around two key flows. One was to Coatbridge in Scotland, formed of anything up to 27 wagons, which required a pair of Class 47s to power it as far as Crewe, where electric traction took over. The second, smaller, train went to Felixstowe and required the use of only a single class 47.

On the pleasant evening of Friday 28 May 1999 the first-mentioned of these services, the 4S81 18:20 Pengam to Coatbridge, is seen with two unidentified Class 47s crossing the 154-yard St Julian's Viaduct between Newport and Caerleon with 20 FFA, FGA, FSA, IKA, KFA and KQAs in tow. The KQAs are well wagons and were constructed to convey 9ft 6in containers over routes where they would not normally be allowed owing to restrictive gauges. They have since been recoded to KTAs.

In the background can be seen the twin towers of Uskmouth 'A' Power Station (since demolished) and the adjacent single stack of Uskmouth 'B' station. Also in this view is the famous Newport Transporter Bridge, one of only two in the country and eight in the world.

**Above:** The demise of Speedlink on 8 July 1991 was one of the most talked about rail decisions of the decade. In hindsight it was, from a business point of view, sadly inevitable. Despite this decimation of the 'part load' aspect of the railway, it refused to die and, as part of the new TRANSRAIL company, small consignments were reinstigated under the 'Enterprise' brand. Although the 'Enterprise' name has now been quietly dropped, the wagonload network, as it is now referred to, continues to flourish under various changes of leadership at EWS/DBS.

These wagonload services convey a fascinating variety of products. For example, this train, the 6M75 16:22 ADJ to Warrington via Llanwern, powered by No 66070, has a BYA and KIA containing steel coil from Llanwern to Liverpool Gladstone Dock, an FCA twin of containerised coal from Onllwyn to Mossend, three JXAs of ferrous scrap from Cattewater to Liverpool Alexandra Dock, and a further KIA and IHA with more steel coil from Port Talbot to Liverpool Gladstone Dock. The location is Ponthir and the date is Friday 22 August 2008.

**Left:** One of the more distinctive trains to run through South Wales was the flow of china clay slurry between Imerys's works at Burngullow in the South West of England and UPM-Kymmene's Caledonian paper mill at Irvine in the South West of Scotland, making it, at the time, the longest single flow on the network. The train, formed of TIA tanks, famously known as 'silver bullets', first started running on 15 March 1989, following the opening of the paper mill. The TIAs were later replaced by new TEAs, 16 of which are pictured here on Wednesday 16 April 2003 behind No 66037 on the 6S55 09:38 WO Burngullow to Irvine.

The last train to run was on 29 January 2008, and this was only used to clear the stocks at Burngullow, the last of the regular trains having run on the 4th of that month. The flow remains on rail, however, as the slurry is now shipped from Brazil to Antwerp in Belgium, then through the Chunnel by train. The first train of 20 ICAs arrived at Dollands Moor on 8 January, resulting in an even longer flow for rail!

**Above:** I have always been interested in train consists and finding out what products are being conveyed, what places they are running between and why they are required. The Freightmaster forum is an invaluable source of information for tying down such details, and after some digging round, this train, Wednesday 22 June 2005's 6M75 19:25 ADJ to Warrington, was found to have been composed of No 66194 hauling one empty TIA from Dow Corning at Barry to British Petroleum (BP) at Immingham for reloading with acrylonitrile; one TTA from Imerys at Burngullow to P. D. Stirling at Mossend conveying china clay slurry; two KVAs conveying tinplate from Corus at Trostre to Harkers at Carlisle; and five FPAs of Russell containers loaded with coal from Celtic Energy at Onllwyn to Deanside Transit in Glasgow.

As can be seen, this one train conveys products from England to Scotland, Wales to Scotland and from Wales to England. 6M75 has conveyed many other traffics over the years, including scrap aluminium, seaweed, foodstuffs and sulphuric acid – space prevents a full list, which would probably take up the entire page!

Some of the trains that run on the network test the steel rails ultrasonically for flaws. When it is considered that one of the flaws it detects is a crack in the rail – and gauge corner cracking was the cause of the awful derailment at Hatfield on 17 October 2000 – it can be seen how important these runs are.

As the trains are limited to 30mph when in testing mode, most run under cover of darkness when paths are more freely available. However, transit moves between places can be undertaken in daylight. Just such an instance is recorded here, when Ultrasonic Test Unit 2 (or UTU 2 for short), formed of No 31190 *Gryphon* top'n'tailing with No 31601 *Bletchley Park 'Station X'*, worked a 4Z08 15:42 St Phillips Marsh to Carnforth. The location is just south of Abergavenny and the date is Wednesday 24 March 2004. The train is entirely in Railtrack's short-lived livery of blue and lime green.

Timber has been a boom-and-bust commodity for railfreight over the years. In South Wales, loading points in the 1990s included Carmarthen and Swansea Burrows, both of which sent traffic to Shotton. Unfortunately this traffic ceased in the early 1990s.

Starting in January 1997, timber traffic could once again be seen in South Wales, but this time of the incoming variety rather than the outgoing. Timber from various loading points in Scotland made its way to ADJ via 'Enterprise' train, whence it ran as a trip to Pontrilas Timber & Builders Merchants' facility at Pontrilas. Ingenious use was made of an existing siding at the south end of Pontrilas loop, which was able to hold five wagons at a time. Such was the popularity of this traffic that it was later extended to a seven-wagon length, with timber also being offloaded at Abergavenny and Hereford as required.

There are five OTAs behind No 66115 as it trundles through Llanvihangel Crucorney with the 6B92 11:30 ADJ to Pontrilas on Friday 16 February 2001. Sadly, after nearly five years, the traffic ceased, the last train running on 21 November 2001.

The 'Westerns', or 'Thousands' as they were also known, were a diesel-hydraulic express loco introduced to the Western Region in 1962 but withdrawn as early as 1977. A number of my friends waxed lyrical about these machines, but as they were before my time I didn't think much of it. However, despite being a life-long Class 37 fan, a trip behind the Diesel Traction Group's (DTG's) painstakingly restored, magical machine from Paddington to Penzance and back 'converted' me from sceptic to believer, and in the process made it rather easy to see how they earned their 'Wizzo' nickname!

On this occasion D1015 *Western Champion*, in D1000's original Golden Ochre livery, makes light work of its coaches while working a Mendip Rail staff day out to Llandudno. The 1Z31 07:05 from Castle Cary was routed up the North & West route and is seen near Llanvihangel on Bank Holiday Monday, 5 May 2003.

In this beautiful snow scene, unidentified units of Classes 153 and 158 are heading north through Llanvihangel with the 06:54 Penzance to Crewe service on Friday 27 February 2004. The 153 is in First North Western's livery of gold and blue and was one of four units transferred to Canton in December 2003, when the Arriva Trains Wales franchise started.

The train has run via the nominally freight-only Maindee Curve, which avoids Newport station.

Under the Speller Act, passenger trains over this curve had been introduced by South Wales & West (SW&W) from the start of the September 1997 timetable, to run in competition with Virgin Cross Country's services, which ran via Birmingham and Cheltenham. The trains proved to be popular, but owing to competition from the about-to-be-formed Greater Western franchise the opportunity for through services was lost and services over the curve ceased on 10 December 2005.

**Above:** On Bank Holiday Monday, 30 May 2005, two Class 175/1s head down Llanvihangel bank with the 17:44 Cardiff to Holyhead service. Normally, pairs of units are unusual over this line, but services were being strengthened in order to take footy fans home from the day's Coca Cola Football League Championship play-off, which saw West Ham United beat Preston Northend by a goal to nil at the Millennium Stadium. All 27 Class 175s (11 two-car units, Nos 175001-175011, and 16 three-car units, Nos 175101-175116) were transferred from First North Western to Arriva Trains Wales under the franchise reorganisation in 2004. However, it took until December 2006 for the fleet to be fully deployed as, prior to that, ATW was contractually obliged to hire 11 of the units back to Trans Pennine Express before the introduction of its new Class 185s.

**Right:** Network Rail contracts DBS and Freightliner Heavy Haul (FHH) to run its National Delivery Service (NDS) trains, linking all parts of the country so that rail, ballast and other materials can be transferred between the required points by scheduled services. The new NDS contracts that began in April 2009 led to the withdrawal of the twice-weekly ADJ to Bescot trains and a consequent increase in the number of trains to Crewe from two to four per week.

The 6M82 18:28 FSX ADJ to Basford Hall is captured running through Walterstone Common on Tuesday 11 August 2009. No 66112 is in charge of an empty rail train consisting of one YEA and 12 JZAs. The distinctive Skirrid Hill dominates the background.

During Wembley's protracted closure for rebuilding between October 2000 and March 2007, Cardiff's truly magnificent Millennium Stadium played host to numerous football matches. Although the sport uses the wrong-shaped ball when compared to the more traditional Welsh sporting pastime, it did have the benefit of bringing many 'special' trains to the nation's capital in connection with the various games.

Ian Riley's pair of Class 37s, Nos 37038 and 37197, are providing power for a 1Z48 08:50 Manchester Piccadilly to Cardiff train, seen coasting past the still-semaphored location of Pontrilas on the North & West route. The 12-coach 'Footex' is being run to the League Cup Final at the Millennium Stadium on Sunday 2 March 2003, on which occasion Liverpool beat Manchester United 2–0.

Ian Riley sold No 37038 to Direct Rail Services (DRS) in April 2003 and then withdrew from the main-line market altogether by selling his remaining four 37s (Nos 37197, 37235, 37261 and 37423) to the West Coast Railway Company in September 2004. In late 2005 Nos 37197 and 37261 were sold to DRS in exchange for its four Class 33s. No 37423 was also then sold to DRS in 2006, but No 37235 remains withdrawn at Carnforth.

Following commissioning and testing, the Portbury Coal Terminal (CT) opened for traffic on 7 January 2002. For the first 5½ years of operation, all coal trains from Portbury were operated by EWS on behalf of its various customers. However, as from Monday 9 July 2007 FHH gained a contract with International Power to operate services to Rugeley Power Station (PS) and a single train a day began operating from that date. To avoid the need for a banking loco up the Lickey incline, loaded trains were booked through the Severn Tunnel and up the Marches route, bringing the sight of FHH coal trains to this line for the first time.

In just the fifth week of operation, No 66563 is whining its way up past Pontrilas with 16 instead of the more normal 19 HXAs, forming the 6Z82 07:00 Portbury CT to Rugeley PS on Wednesday 8 August 2007.

From 18 November 2008 another contract was gained to take coal between Portbury and Fiddlers Ferry, meaning that paths then existed for up to six FHH coal trains a day along the N&W route. The actual number of services per day depends upon customer requirements and in early December 2008 the split was two to Rugeley and two to Fiddlers, while in March 2009 there were six trains to just Rugeley.

In February 2000 two Multi Purpose Vehicles (MPVs) were disbanded and the power units of each vehicle re-formed to make a power twin set, so that trials of a new concept (in Britain) called a Freight Multiple Unit (FMU) could be undertaken. The first runs were for Freightliner between Barking and Southampton.

The second trial in 2001 saw FMUs take Bulmers products from Hereford to Willesden for distribution in London. The third set of trials in 2002 saw it split into three parts: the first ran between Hams Hall and Tilbury, the second between Tilbury and Hereford, this time taking in raw materials, and the third between Widnes and Mossend. The most recent set of trials in 2005 saw them sandwich a rake of OTAs, taking timber from Aberystwyth to Chirk.

This photo illustrates the second set of trials. Power twin MPV Nos DR98904 and DR98906 and four FKAs, each loaded with one 45-foot Seaco container, arrive at Hereford before reversing into the yard, then reversing again to take the branch down to the Bulmers factory. The train is the 6Z79 11:53 MWFO Willesden to Hereford, and the date is Wednesday 1 August 2001.

Despite these many trials and announcements of success, and despite many rumours, no commercial FMUs have been ordered and the project seems to have been relegated to the back burner.

The Welsh Assembly Government (WAG) has provided many millions of pounds to improve train services in Wales over the years, including the funding or part funding of infrastructure improvements, or the financing of extra units to run strengthened, lengthened, additional or new services. Unfortunately, most of these improvements go unnoticed by the public and even by most enthusiasts, as they involve the use of units. However, one such innovation that has caught the eye was the introduction of a new, fast, sub-4½-hour service linking Holyhead and Cardiff, unofficially, and perhaps a little harshly, known as the 'WAG Express'.

ATW, the Wrexham Shropshire & Marylebone Railway and Grand Union all bid to run the contract, but due to the short timescales involved it was ATW that introduced its 'Premier' service from Monday 15 December 2008 using No 57314 top'n'tailing with No 57315. As from Monday 9 February 2009 the train was booked for just a single loco. However, top'n'tailed or double-headed, combinations can still sometimes be seen in order to swap over the spare loco based at Canton. On just such an occasion, the only two locos displaying the full ATWP-branded livery, Nos 57314 and 57315, work the 1W91 16:15 Cardiff to Holyhead service past Onibury on Wednesday 9 September 2009.

In addition to the freight operations mentioned elsewhere in this book, Cotswold Rail once ran its own railtours, marketed under the Heartland Rail banner. This was followed by the lease of Nos 43070 and 43087, after which they purchased most of the Blue Pullman stock. It is fair, but unfortunate, to say that, in 2007, Heartland Rail cancelled and postponed at least as many tours as it ran. The buying out of the 'Steamy Affairs' operator proved to be a step too far, and following its liquidation on 19 February 2008 no railtours have been run by Cotswold since that time.

As well as running its own tours, Cotswold also provided power for other operators, as is the case here when Compass Railtours' 'The Heart of Wales Explorer' used Cotswold's uniquely liveried locos Nos 47714, in the defunct Anglia scheme, and 47818, in the replacement ONE colours. Behind them are nine Virgin Mk 3s, one FGW sleeper coach and Driving Van Trailer (DVT) No 82134, which are providing a comfortable means of transport for passengers on the 1Z63 06:05 Preston to Cardiff service via the Heart of Wales line. The ensemble is seen running through Craven Arms station on Saturday 29 April 2006 just before swinging off the North & West route and onto the Heart of Wales line proper.

The Pontypool & Blaenavon Railway (P&BR) lies adjacent to the wonderful Big Pit mining museum. This short (half-mile) but steep (1 in 40) line between Furnace Sidings and Whistle Inn is not only the highest preserved line in Wales, but is located in a World Heritage Site. The railway is currently being extended 1¼ miles southwards to the former Blaenavon High Level station, which the P&BR will open in 2010. Further extensions are planned to within Big Pit itself, then, longer term, to Varteg, Talywain and Wainfelin in the south, and Waunavon and Brynmawr in the north.

No 37216 was sold by EWS from Motherwell and transported to Kingsbury for scrap, before being bought by a P&BR board member. The loco arrived at the P&BR on Friday 20 July 2007 and was in working order just eight days later. Its first run in preservation was on Saturday 28 July, propelling two coaches up the gradient as the 11:30 departure from Furnace Sidings to Whistle Inn. The following day, at the very end of the weekend's diesel gala, No 37216 rumbles downgrade from Whistle Inn with a demonstration freight of two Lowmacs, one Dogfish and a Shark brake-van.

The last ever BR 'Peak' working into South Wales took place on 31 July 1988 when No 45141 worked the Sundays-only 15:35 Leeds to Cardiff service. The loco returned the next day on the 1O41 19:43 Cardiff to Southampton parcels train as far as Bristol Temple Meads, where it then picked up the 1E94 21:40 Bristol to Newcastle service. The loco was switched off for the last time just three days later, making it the very last 'Peak' in ordinary revenue-earning service.

It took until 18 July 2001 for a Class 45 to appear on the main line again, when Fragonset's No 45112 *Royal Army Ordnance Corps* worked a test train, just prior to working a railtour a few days later. It has since remained the only Class 45 to work on the main line in the privatised era and is seen here with 13 coaches in tow forming the 1Z30 20:15 Minehead to Cardiff service on Saturday 6 December 2003, pausing at Newport to let passengers off Pathfinder Tours' 'Dunster by Candlelight and Minehead' railtour.

No 45112 was transferred to Nemesis Rail when FMR went into administration in December 2006; however, its outings since then have been few and far between, and this picture is thought to have recorded its last working (so far) to South Wales.

The EWS Saloon train (as it is officially known), or Keith Heller's toy train (as it is very unofficially known), or the Scooby train (as it is known by enthusiasts), was unveiled at Toton on 19 October 2004 as a means for entertaining existing and potential customers and clients, undertaking staff trips, charity work, managerial and special functions, being offered for use as a hospitality train or mobile office, as well as undertaking operational and engineering inspections.

Its first visit to South Wales came on Tuesday 17 May 2005 when No 82146 led coaches Nos 10546, 10211, 11039 and 'skip' 67029 to form the 1Z05 07:22 Paddington to Cardiff service.

The train ran as empty coaching stock (ECS) back to Newport as a 5Z05 11:00 from Cardiff, was turned on the Maindee triangle and went to Godfrey Road stabling sidings, where it is pictured after arrival. For operational reasons the DVT tends to lead for the majority of the trips and the turn on the Maindee triangle was to continue this aspect of its operation.

Godfrey Road stabling point closed on 27 May 2006 and its duties were transferred to a new set of three short dead-end sidings at ADJ from the same day. This allowed the construction of Newport's Platform 4 to take place, which has subsequently changed this view for ever.

EWS, and later DBS, have long held the contract with the Ministry of Defence (MoD) to move munitions, equipment and vehicles around the various rail-connected sites in Britain. In the 1980s Welsh sites at Trecwn, Newton Noyes, Caerwent and Glascoed all received and dispatched regular traffic, some of it going to Newport and Barry Docks for export. However, 20 years later the first three depots had shut altogether and Glascoed's rail link had closed. Despite this, the latter's traffic continued to run by rail to either Kineton or Longtown, being dispatched via Freightliner's terminal at Pengam and, when that shut, its replacement at Wentloog.

No 37308 has two VBA barrier wagons on either side of two KFA container wagons, forming the 4B24 14:04 FX 'Q' service from Didcot Yard to Wentloog, and is drifting through Gaer Junction on Tuesday 24 June 2003.

MoD traffic in the form of tanks and other combat vehicles flourishes in Wales. As well as the 'regular' destinations of Haverfordwest and, to a lesser extent, Pembroke Dock, a new destination has been tried with a number of trains being run to Cwmbargoed in October 1998 and June 2002 to serve the ranges up at Sennybridge in the Brecon Beacons.

When the yards at Severn Tunnel Junction closed on 11 October 1987, their duties were split up and transferred to various Network Yards (NY) at Gloucester, East Usk and Cardiff Tidal. Over the years the last-named has lost its 'Enterprise' duties. Gloucester NY has shut altogether and, owing to complaints by nearby residents about the noise, the duties of East Usk were transferred to ADJ. ADJ remained the principal yard in Newport for wagonload traffic until it closed on 5 April 2009, its duties then being split between a revitalised East Usk Yard and Llanwern Exchange Sidings. However,

following the destruction by fire of East Usk signal box early in the morning of Sunday 19 April 2009, ADJ reopened just two weeks after it shut!

Here we see the classic view at the north end of ADJ on Tuesday 6 May 2003 as a rather tatty No 37798 takes out 27 engineer's wagons forming the 7M12 18:17 TThO ADJ to Bescot train. The lengthy consist includes ten wooden-bodied OBAs, ZDAs and metal-bodied OCAs, seven YSA/YWAs and ten more OBA/OCAs. The line to Newport Docks sweeps off to the left.

**Above:** Engineer's trains can provide a rich assortment of wagons in a wide variety of liveries. On Thursday 15 April 1999, and far from its intended express mail duties, No 47584 *The Locomotive and Carriage Institution 1911* has one Mainline blue-liveried ZUA 'Shark', four yellow YSA 'Salmon's, one 'Dutch'-liveried YGB 'Seacow', one Loadhaul-liveried OCA and five-EWS liveried MHA 'Coalfish's behind it, as it enters ADJ Yard on a special from Swindon.

Partially hidden behind the first three wagons of the train are a ZFV 'Dogfish', two YCV 'Turbots', a ZDA and a condemned ZBV 'Grampus'. Randomly, behind them is a green Railtrack PNA, a Transrail grey ZCA and an S&T red/yellow ZDA. The loaded OTAs of timber beyond will be for Pontrilas.

Instead of the previous 'cast offs', engineer's trains are nowadays getting their own dedicated new-build stock for the various trains carrying spoil, ballast, sleepers, rails, track panels and now switches. For those interested in delving deeper into the railway scene, there is a rich tapestry of workings, wagons and wonderfulness to be explored within the engineering division.

**Right:** Aluminium was transported to South Wales in vast quantities for Novelis's (formerly Alcan's) hot rolling plant at Rogerstone, just outside Newport. In the mid 1990s aluminium was transported by Freightliner from Fort William to Pengam and by EWS from Lynemouth to the Wolverhampton Steel Terminal, where it was then roaded to the plant from those locations.

Following the opening of the bulk handling terminal in Newport Docks (now the coal terminal), EWS revised its service from 14 February 2000 to run the aluminium to this point instead, later combining it with the flow from Fort William, which it won from Freightliner in January 2005.

The unloading of the aluminium was soon switched within Newport Docks from the bulk terminal to a dedicated hardstanding on the SIMS branch. On Tuesday 5 June 2007, just a few yards short of its new destination, No 66142 arrives at Newport Docks with its 11 BDAs and BEAs of aluminium slab.

Unfortunately, the recession meant that Novelis announced the closure of its Rogerstone plant on 4 March 2009, and the last inbound train of aluminium arrived in the docks on Tuesday 7 April.

Rail traffic to and from Newport Docks has increased steadily over the past ten years using seven (now six) loading points within the complex. Inbound traffic has included aluminium from Fort William and Lynemouth; scrap EMUs from Shoeburyness; shredded scrap from Beeston, St Blazey, Handsworth Queen's Head and Exeter; coal from Parc Slip and New Cumnock for blending; coal from Cwmbargoed for export; steel products from Port Talbot, Llanwern and Shotton for export; fly ash from Uskmouth; munitions; 'Nightstar' coaches for export to Canada; and GIF (Gestor de Infraestructuras Ferroviarias) Class 58s for export to Spain.

Outbound traffic from Newport Docks has included stone to Leeds and Elstow; imported rail to Eastleigh; imported coal to power stations at Uskmouth, Aberthaw, Didcot, Rugeley and Ferrybridge;

blended coal to Rugby Cement Works, Tavistock Junction (for Plymstock Cement Works), Westbury Cement Works and Foxton (for Barrington Cement Works); munitions; steel slab to Llanwern and Port Talbot Steelworks; steel coil to Llanwern; iron ore to Llanwern; intermodal traffic to Wembley; scrap to Cardiff Tidal; and (of course) all except one of every Class 66 and 67 imported into this country.

On Saturday 23 September 2006, in the coal terminal on the south-west side of the south dock, No 66062 has arrived with the 6F52 09:30 from Uskmouth PS and is running round its 33 HAAs, HDAs and HMAs, which are to be loaded with coal to depart at 13:00 as the 6F53 to Aberthaw.

Still in Newport Docks, the subject of this illustration, taken on Saturday 23 September 2006, is incoming steel coil from Llanwern, which is being reversed into No 7 shed by No 60020. No 7 shed was (officially) opened for steel coil imports and exports on 20 October 1997, and gratifyingly has seen almost continuous use ever since.

The Class 60 had actually arrived with an empty slab working and was being used as a 'super shunter' while waiting for its train to be loaded on the wharf. The line to the left is to Hargreaves siding, which has seen inward coal traffic and outward blended coal/petroleum coke trains to a variety of cement works.

Railtours are a popular countrywide phenomenon, ranging from the enthusiast special (using freight or heritage locomotives; covering freight branches; or visiting normally unit-only destinations) to the ordinary public day-trip variety (visiting interesting places like York or the Eden Project) and the luxury end of the market (such as the Venice Simplon Orient Express (VSOE), 'Northern Belle' or 'Royal Scotsman'). Some are combinations of these, such as Fishwick's 'The Mid Wales Borderer' railtour on Saturday 19 July 2008, which used Martin Walker's 'heritage' diesel No 55022 *Royal Scots Grey* together with the West Coast Railway Company's No 57601, to visit the highly scenic Heart of Wales Line.

The train ran as the 1Z55 06:15 Blackpool North to Cardiff service, which should have ensured that No 55022 led throughout. However, a points problem at Hendy Junction meant that the train had to go down to Morlais Junction and reverse in order to gain access to the Swansea District Line and run to Cardiff. Rather than performing a double run-round at ADJ, the train was turned on the Maindee triangle and is pictured on its way back west as the 5Z56 15:05 Cardiff to Canton.

Beneath the sixth coach is Ebbw Junction, where the lines to Park Junction, Machen and Ebbw Vale diverge; they will be the subject of our next detour.

Park Junction was once the converging point of no fewer than five lines, as well as having a pair of 'through' lines behind the signal box. Although the line to Maesglas Junction closed in the early 1980s, the lines to Gaer Junction, Ebbw Junction, Machen and Ebbw Vale remain.

Following the closure of Ebbw Vale tinplate and galvanising works, the last remaining Western Valley line above Newport became redundant. As part of the package to help alleviate the massive redundancies this would cause, the Welsh Assembly Government undertook to restore passenger services to the town, withdrawn as long ago as 30 April 1962.

Prior to the engineering work taking place, the last non-engineering train to traverse the length of the line was on Thursday 29 June 2006, when No 901002, comprising Nos 977693 (ex-53222) and 977694 (ex-53338), also known as 'Iris II' or 'Lab 19', formed a 2Z02 09:37 East Usk Yard to Park Junction service.

**Left:** Under its various previous owners, the quarry at Machen has long been a source of ballast for the railway until it unfortunately ceased in March 2009. As well as the limestone that is quarried here, gritstone from Hanson's Craig yr Hesg and Gelligaer quarries is transported here by road and loaded onto rail wagons. The gritstone trains have been run via Westbury to variously Crawley, West Drayton, Allington and Ardingly, using Class 56s, 58s, 59/0s, 59/1s, 59/2s, 60s, 66/0s, 66/5s and 66/9s!

The 59/0s and 59/1s are not common visitors to Machen, so this shot taken on Saturday 11 August 2007 of No 59101 *Village of Whatley* is a pleasing one to have. It has 18 JHAs in tow, with the stone (on this occasion) bound for Allington, initially running as the 6C80 14:10 SO Machen to Westbury, where it would be added to one of the 'jumbo' trains to Acton before final distribution to its destination.

The train is crossing Bassaleg Viaduct, which, since 2000, has become the oldest remaining working railway viaduct in Britain. It was built in 1826 as part of the Rumney tramroad between the Rhymney Iron Works and a junction with the Monmouthshire Railway & Canal Company's line at Pye Corner (Bassaleg), situated immediately to the right of this picture. Conversion from tramroad to railway didn't occur until 30 years later, and apart from some obvious and rather ugly signs of strengthening it has seen continuous use for some 184 years.

Machen Quarry has long had a requirement for a shunting locomotive. When I first started visiting in the early 1990s, F. C. Hipberd & Co Ltd's 'Planet' loco, No 3890, was out of use and Sentinel 0-4-0 diesel No 10222 was being used instead.

However, as it was a vacuum-brake-only loco it was replaced by D2199 from the South Yorkshire Railway in November 2000, seen here six months later on Monday 30 April 2001, loading up ZCAs with railway ballast.

The 03 failed catastrophically on Sunday 19 March 2006 and was replaced by '08296' (actually the former D3955/08787) from Whatley, which was still there as this book went to press. The Sentinel is currently resident at the Llanelli & Mynydd Mawr Railway headquarters in Cynheidre.

**Left:** The South Wales Valleys scene is typified by this view of No 60065 *Kinder Low* and 17 BCAs and BLAs of hot rolled coil making slow progress up alongside the terraced streets of Llanhilleth on Sunday 13 October 1998 with the 6B71 09:38 Margam Terminal Complex (TC) to Ebbw Vale via Llanwern.

The last coil train to Ebbw Vale ran on 25 June 2002 as the 6B09 07:05 from Llanwern, and the last tinplate train ran from the works on 12 July, a week after official closure.

BR traffic to Ebbw Vale was once exchanged in the gargantuan mass of sidings at Waunllwyd. However, this land was required for use by the 1992 Ebbw Vale Garden Festival, so a new set of sidings, known as Victoria sidings, was opened for use in January 1989.

The difference in level between the Ebbw Vale works and the new exchange sidings required a switchback line on a ferocious upward gradient for loaded trains. This is seen to good effect on Sunday 10 June 2001 as *Gillian* (nearest) and *Tracey* (at the head of the train) are seen top'n'tailing 10 BCAs and BLAs of coil up the line and into the headshunt before reversing it into the works. The coil had only just been brought into the south sidings by No 60059 *Swinden Dalesman* as part of that day's 6B76 15:10 SunO Margam to Ebbw Vale, one of three regular Sunday trains to the works at that time.

Ebbw Vale shut on 5 July 2002, its tinplating duties being transferred to Trostre and its galvanising duties to Llanwern and Shotton. The site has now been flattened and awaits redevelopment.

**Left:** The last weekday passenger train to run at night in South Wales is currently the 23:50 Paddington to Cardiff, arriving at 02:31 the next morning – except for Fridays train, which arrives at 02:18 Saturday morning. On Saturdays, the last train to run is the 23:09 from Gloucester, arriving in Cardiff at 00:34 Sunday morning. This train, an unidentified class 170, is pictured at Duffryn under the light of a full moon on Sunday 3 August 2009.

During the summer of 2009, engineering possessions were being taken Saturday nights to erect new signal gantries in the Newport area and the possession of all 4 lines had to wait until this train had run. However, the possession on the main lines had already been given, which explains why this train is running over the down relief instead of the more normal down main.

**Above:** In 1994 the ban preventing preserved diesels from running on the BR network was finally lifted and the first loco to be recertified for main-line use was Pete Waterman's D172. Registered as

No 89472, the former No 46035 and 97403 made a triumphant return on 18 August 1994, running along the North Wales coast with a test trip.

Pete Waterman was contracted to run a number of extras for, amongst other things, the 1999 Rugby World Cup, including this, the 08:41 Crewe to Cardiff, for the game between Wales and Manu Samoa. On that occasion No 47705 *Guy Fawkes* failed with a speedo defect and was rescued by Class 46 D172 *Ixion*, and the pair are seen ambling along through Coedkernew on Thursday 14 October 1999 en route to the day's festivities. The speedo was fixed at Canton, enabling the 46 to return light engine and the 47 to work the return unassisted.

No 46035 worked what turned out to be its last main-line tour on 28 June 2003. Following a turn at the Severn Valley Railway Diesel Gala in October 2003, the loco went to Leeds Midland Road for an 'E' exam that was never completed and, sadly, it has remained out of use ever since.

## Cardiff area: main line, valleys and branches

**Above:** In 1986 and 1987 six Class 37s were converted by BR as test beds for a potential Class 38 project. Four 37s received Mirlees Blackstone MB275T engines and became Nos 37901 to 37904, while two more received Ruston RK270T engines and were renumbered Nos 37905 and 37906. They were based at Canton for their entire working lives, initially being part of the Metals sector. When TRANSRAIL came into being in 1994, they migrated to working other services including coal, oil and construction trains, as is illustrated by this working.

As part of the construction of a Waste Water Treatment Works to the south of Cardiff, trains of crushed blast furnace slag were moved from both Llanwern and Port Talbot Steelworks to Cardiff Docks, where the slag was unloaded and transported the short distance to the site by road.

Here, in the first week of operation, No 37906 has 37 empty MEAs ready for refilling as the 6Z52 11:05 Cardiff Docks to Llanwern on Saturday 29 August 1998. On the left of the picture now lies the South Wales International Freightliner Terminal, otherwise known as Wentloog, the demic bridge having been removed to enable its construction.

**Right:** Since the creation of Freightliner Heavy Haul in 1999, it has operated several freight contracts in South Wales, namely propylene to Baglan Bay and contaminated spoil from the same place; coal to Fifoots; the dragging of HST power cars to Landore; various engineer's trains; ballast from Machen; gritstone from Tower, Neath Abbey Wharf (AWF), Machen and Moreton on Lugg to some 13 different destinations; sand to Neath AWF; scrap EMUs and stock to Caerwent; scrap to Tidal and Newport Docks; cement to Uskmouth; wagon moves to and from Cathays, Wentloog, Canton and Aberthaw Cement Works; a trial load of stone to Llantrisant; and the inevitable railtours, 'Ruggex' specials and route learners to most parts of South Wales. Phew!

FHH has also operated services that start and finish outside Wales, but that travel through the country during their journey. Such trains have included coal from Portbury and Avonmouth to Rugeley and Fiddlers Ferry and cars from Portbury to Bathgate.

FHH replaced EWS as hauliers of Aggregate Industries (AI) stone trains countrywide from 1 April 2005. Having been loaded at Neath AWF the day before, No 66560 has 20 FLHH JGAs behind it as the 6Z28 08:31 Pengam to Theale. The train is pictured less than 30 seconds into its journey, rumbling over the Rumney River bridge on Saturday 25 August 2007.

Rover Way bridge in Cardiff has always been a popular spot for enthusiasts. Once overlooking the former Pengam sorting sidings, they were replaced by a new Freightliner depot that opened on 8 June 1967. However, time marches inevitably onwards and the last train left Pengam Freightliner Terminal (FLT) on Tuesday 13 February 2001, the facility being replaced by Wentloog a couple of miles up the line.

Pengam sidings, however, remained in use, and in them are No 66174 and nine JIA/JIB Polybulks forming the 6V70 11:50 TFO Cliffe Vale to Tidal train. At Tidal the train will pick up any empty scrap wagons required for Cattewater or St Blazey and head south later that evening.

In the distance is No 66037 with 15 KEAs, having just run round its 6B07 12:46 TFO Waterston to Tidal empty stone train. The date is Tuesday 7 June 2005 and one has to appreciate the coincidence of two 'Tuesday Friday Only' trains meeting at Pengam at the same time.

Photograph number *13* of the film, taken on Friday *13* June 2008, shows No 66121 with *13* SPAs in tow as the 6B64 08:10 WFO Tidal to ADJ, leaving the branch from Cardiff Docks at Pengam. Although this wasn't my *13*th attempt at photographing this train, it seemed like it, as previous efforts had been thwarted by various combinations of early running, late running, no running, traffic jams and cloud more times than I considered absolutely necessary. The wire coil is destined for Mossend by way of that evening's 6M75 to Warrington, and from there by the 6M65 to Carlisle and 6S65 to Mossend. Other destinations for coil from the reopened Celsa works have been Colnbrook and Rotherham.

One of the more unpredictable trains to track down has been the stone empties to Cardiff Docks. The train has run once every one to two weeks for a few months at a time since September 2002. It is made more interesting by the fact that it has provided the only sight of the Lafarge (formerly Redland) Self Discharge Train in the principality, with of course a few minor exceptions.

On Tuesday 27 September 2005 No 66055 is captured approaching Splott Junction between Cardiff Tidal and Cardiff Docks with the 6V45 10:26 TO Banbury to Cardiff Docks. There are 10 PGA/PHAs, a KJA and 30 more PHAs behind it, which will be loaded with stone from Hafod Quarry and taken that evening to (in this instance) Mountsorrel for unloading.

Currently, scrap trains for Cardiff Tidal sidings can be destined for one of three unloading points in the vicinity. Celsa's Tremorfa works has two of these locations within its boundaries, where the scrap is recycled to make rebar. European Metal Recycling (EMR) has the other siding at its Dowlais Wharf in Cardiff Docks where the scrap is exported. The former rail connection to the SIMS plant has been out of use for some years.

Between February 2008 and February 2010, Celsa was receiving or had received scrap by rail from Attercliffe, Barry Docks, Beeston, Brierley Hill, Handsworth EMR, Handsworth Queen's Head, Hitchin, Kingsbury, Lincoln Terrace, Newport Docks, Rotherham Booths, Rotherham Masborough, Saltley, Shipley, St Blazey, Stockton, Swindon, Thorney Mill and Tyne Dock.

Over the same period, EMR also received scrap by rail from just its facilities at Swindon and Cattewater in Plymouth. In this view, No 08752 has brought 12 SSAs out of the EMR siding and is seen approaching Splott Junction heading towards Cardiff Tidal on Tuesday 6 May 2003. The empties will return to Cattewater by way of wagonload services to ADJ and Tavistock Junction yard. All remaining SSAs were put into store in February 2009 and the traffic was run using JNAs until it ceased later in the year.

Following the introduction of Virgin Cross Country's 'Voyager' fleet in 2001, there was a reduction in the number of HST power cars required for service, and they were therefore made available by their leasing companies to other operators. Railtrack took advantage of this and purchased three power cars (Nos 43013, 43014 and 43062) in order to form a 'New Measurement Train' (NMT), which, following Railtrack's collapse, was continued by Network Rail with enthusiasm. The NMT first began operation on 5 June 2003 and first visited Wales 16 days later. Over the years new power cars and coaches have

been added and replaced, so that it has run in South Wales with anywhere between four and seven coaches and with a variety of traction.

On Friday 3 October 2008 Nos 43062 *John Armitt* and 43014 sandwich five Mk 3s as they head east out of Cardiff with the 1Z20 05:42 Old Oak Common to Derby Railway Technical Centre (RTC) via Swansea.

Some of the coal carried by rail in the middle of the 20th century was for the railway's own purposes, being the fuel required by its various steam engines. Today, in much the same way, the gas oil required by diesels, is still carried by rail from two supply points at Fawley and Lindsey to various depots around the country.

In 2008, gas oil for Arriva Trains Wales at Canton and DBS at Margam came from Fawley, originally as a block train and then later via 'Enterprise'. Unfortunately the Margam portion ceased to run in 2009 when the fuelling point was moved to the yard as part of the depots lingering death and it is currently supplied by road tanker. The Canton fuel has, since being conveyed by 'Enterprise', operated first as a twice, and then as a once weekly morning trip to and from ADJ.

On Friday 28 July 2006 No 37417 *Richard Trevithick* was the rostered power for the 6B98 08:39 WFO Canton to ADJ, conveying just three discharged TTAs. The train is erupting out of Cardiff, passing under Tyndall Street footbridge.

**Above:** The fourth Rugby World Cup was held in Wales in 1999, and the final on Saturday 6 November saw Australia triumph over France by 35 points to 12.

One of the many extra trains to Cardiff that day produced the country's most notable working of that year. Making only the class's eighth visit to South Wales, Deltic Preservation Society's (DPS's) D9009 *Alycidon* hauled the five-coach 'Queen of Scots' set from London Victoria to Cardiff. The special returned that evening as the 1Z12 17:50 from Cardiff, seen here picking up its few passengers at the west end of Platform 2.

Most of the gathered photographers expected it to stop much further up the platform, and by the time the dash through the crowded platforms had been completed, the train was ready to go and this meant several of the photographers present ended up missing the shot altogether. As it was, this lucky 8-second exposure was my only effort before the train quickly left.

**Right:** Not far from Cardiff Central is the revitalised Cardiff Bay area, served by a short branch from Cardiff Queen Street. This marks the start of our tour around the Cardiff Valleys.

At least 11 liveries have been seen in the Cardiff Valleys on Canton-allocated Class 142, 143 and 150/2 units since they were introduced in the 1980s. This particular 'Times are Changing' scheme was unveiled in November 2005 to promote the fact that a standard-pattern timetable was to be introduced from December of that year, giving regular clock-face departures at each of the stations on the network. The livery was carried by Nos 143601, 143609, 158841 and this unit, 153323, which is seen entering Cardiff Bay station forming the 2B28 10:10 from Cardiff Queen Street on Friday 8 September 2006.

And seeing as you asked, the liveries have been Provincial, Regional Railways, Valley Lines, GMPTE, Valley Fun Day, Bristol, Anglia, Scot Rail, Wessex, Times are Changing and ATW.

**Above:** There have been many special passenger trains around the Cardiff Valleys over the years, too numerous to mention here. One such set of specials occurred on Sunday 31 May 1998 as part of the Barry Transport Festival. Nos 37211, in the Civil Engineer's 'Dutch' livery, and 37411 *Ty Hafan* in EWS, top'n'tailed four of 'Tom's Tarts' ('Deborah', 'Wendy', 'Felicity' and 'Georgina') around the network, starting at Rhymney and visiting Barry Island, Aberdare and Coryton during the course of the day. In this view the 2Z01 11:20 Barry Island to Coryton train is passing through Rhiwderin on the single-track Coryton branch.

**Right:** The 'Bristol' livery was introduced by Wessex Trains on its Class 143s to promote various aspects of the area in which they operated. Some of the units were then transferred to Canton and widened that promotional aspect, albeit unintentionally! No 143623 is in charge of the 13:42 Bargoed to Penarth service leaving Ystrad Mynach on Tuesday 1 November 2005.

At approximately 20:25 on Monday 1 August 2005 No 37408 *Loch Rannoch* ran away from the headshunt at Rhymney and crashed into a set of coaches, which then also damaged No 37425. For the rest of that week units substituted on rush-hour trains. However, to cover for the loss, ATW hired in Riviera Trains locos and stock, starting on Monday 8 August, when No 47839 worked the 2R42 17:11 Cardiff to Rhymney service. No 37425 returned to traffic on Monday 5 September and No 47847 worked what everyone thought was going to be the last Class 47-hauled train from Rhymney the next morning as the 2F05 07:17 departure down to Cardiff.

However, as we all know, the 'Rhymneys' kept on coming back – as did the Riviera 47s!

They worked for a few days in November 2005 and again for one week, starting on Monday 20 February 2006 (the famous 're-start' of the Rhymney loco-hauled trains).

In this instance it is No 47839, in Riviera's own livery of Oxford Blue, that is providing the power for the 2F06 07:39 Rhymney to Cardiff Central service on a pleasant Thursday 11 August 2005. The train has left Pontlottyn and is heading south towards its next stop at Tir-Phil. The last Brush Type 4 to work in the valleys was the West Coast Railway Company's No 47854 on Saturday 4 March 2006, when it worked the 2F10 07:44 Rhymney to Cardiff train.

Back in the days of the irrepressible Ed Burkhardt, when nothing seemed impossible, one of the new services to appear in Wales was a flow of tinplate to Rhymney, Impress Metal Packaging. After a trial in July the first train to this works was on Monday 5 October 1998 and I was told at the time that it was the first train to serve the plant for 22 years. On this noteworthy occasion No 37719 provided the power for seven IWB Ferrywagons as the 6Z33 21:33 from Margam. This was the maximum length for the train, being limited by the run-round loop in the works. Even then the train had to be split into rakes of two for unloading in the even shorter siding in the warehouse. The 42 coils of tinplate from both Trostre and Ebbw Vale were soon unloaded and the train departed back to Margam on Tuesday 6 October as the 6Z34 03:40 from Rhymney.

Sadly, Impress closed its works and the last train ran on 15 September 2000. It was impressive that rail could compete with road in taking tinplate from Ebbw Vale to Rhymney. The rail journey via Margam was around 111 miles, while the road journey was less than 10!

The last remaining bi-directional semaphore post in South Wales – and, it is thought, on the whole of Railtrack – was on the 'City Line' between Cardiff and Radyr via Ninian Park. The post contained Radyr Junction's fixed Up Branch Distant, Radyr Quarry Junction's Down Home and Radyr Quarry Junctions Up Starter, which is in the 'off' position.

When No 143606 was seen on Saturday 25 April 1998 working the 17:02 Coryton to Radyr service, the post had less than a month to live before being demolished and replaced by colour light signalling as part of the resignalling scheme that, between January 1997 and October 1998, saw the duties of Walnut Tree, Maesmawr, Llandaff, Radyr Quarry, Radyr Junction, Pontypridd and Porth signal boxes transferred to a new Valleys Radyr panel.

The intense coverage that the Rhymney loco-hauled trains received was out of all proportion to the many other services that used to ply the Cardiff Valleys network on a daily basis. This was a pity, as there have been considerable changes in infrastructure, signalling, unit types and liveries over the years. One such livery that can no longer be seen anywhere is the former Wessex colour scheme. Eight Class 150/2s were transferred from Wessex Trains to ATW in December 2006 and they could regularly be found working in all corners of the Valleys network. Here No 150241 *The Tarka Belle* has charge of the 2Y47 12:22 Aberdare to Barry Island service, accelerating away from its Abercynon North stop on Thursday 25 January 2007. The line to Merthyr Tydfil heads steeply up the valley on the right.

This scene is now much changed. The line the unit is on has gone, to be replaced by a new track to the east side of the station; the platform length has been considerably reduced to allow a diamond crossover to be installed at the north end; a new ramped access has been created; the former GWR signal box has been demolished and replaced with a new panel box nearby; and new colour light signals have replaced the former semaphores. Happily, though, the lower-quadrant pegs have found a new home on the Gloucestershire Warwickshire Railway.

The story of Tower Colliery and its workers' buyout is the stuff of legend among the Welsh mining community and is well known throughout the entire country. Closed by British Coal as uneconomic on Friday 22 April 1994, 239 of the workforce contributed £8,000 each from their redundancy pay and reopened the pit on 3 January 1995. They then ran the pit, at a profit, for the next 13 years until it closed on Friday 25 January 2008, becoming the last mine in Wales to use winding headgear as part of its operations. During that time Tower dispatched coal by rail to St Blazey, Immingham, Llanwern, Fort William and Doncaster, but by far the bulk of the production went to Aberthaw Power Station.

Here No 66207 has 18 empty HTAs behind it, slowly entering the loading pad over the weighbridge as the 6C46 10:50 MFSX Aberthaw PS to Tower Colliery. The last train of Tower coal ran from the site on Friday 4 January 2008, with the exception of one (loaded) crippled wagon, which was dispatched 17 days later.

However, the future for the branch is still healthy. At the time of writing coal trains are still loaded here, using coal from the Aberpergwm mine and Nant Y Mynydd opencast in the Neath Valley. It is hoped that some time after this book reaches the shelves, Tower will start opencast operations on the site, bringing further trains to the Cynon and Taff valleys.

For many years in the 1990s two companies carried out weedkilling duties all over the rail network. One, Hunslet Barclay, used six Class 20/9s to top'n'tail its trains as required around the network. The other, AgrEvo, used hired-in traction.

Although the Hunslet Barclay train had appeared in previous years, in 1998 it was the turn of the AgrEvo train, formed on this occasion by No 37517, four KCAs, three TTAs and No 37114

*City of Worcester*. It is working the 7Z07 18:10 Cardiff Taff Vale Sidings to Treherbert, Aberdare, Rhymney, Cardiff Bay, Coryton and Penarth. This shot was obtained at Treherbert on Saturday 18 April 1998.

Multi Purpose Vehicles (MPVs) took over the weedkilling duties from the following year and have plied the network, unloved and mostly unseen, ever since.

The popular red and green Valley Lines livery applied to the Class 150/2s differed enormously from that applied to the 143s and all but one of the 142s. The last Class 142 to retain Regional Railways livery was No 142081, which in February 2003 was repainted into the 150/2 version of the livery to commemorate Richard Trevithick's 200th anniversary, and that unit is seen here working the 08:01 Aberdare to Barry Island service. No 143604, in the more 'normal' Valley Lines livery, is seen in the distance forming the 08:45 Barry Island to Aberdare service. The units are pictured at Cogan Junction on Thursday 20 May 2004.

The problem of 'leaves on the line' was the subject of much derision by an uninformed and unknowing general public when it first hit the headlines in the late 1990s. However, the problem is akin to black ice on the roads and for the drivers is frighteningly real. Each year Network Rail spends millions of pounds combating the problem using a mixture of MPVs and Sandite-fitted locos as appropriate. From 2003 Network Rail (NR) introduced Rail Head Treatment Trains (RHTT), which either singly or in combination use Sandite (a sticky gel-like substance) and/or water-jetting to clear the rails of the leaf mulch.

It wasn't until 2004 that the first RHTTs were based in Wales, using hired-in EWS Class 37s. This was in fact the only year that 37s appeared on these trains, as EWS Class 66s have been the unflinching form of motive power in South Wales for all subsequent years. On Sunday 24 October 2004 Nos 37684 *Peak National Park* and 37692 *Didcot Depot*, in its unique pale blue livery, are seen sandwiching two FEAs forming the 6Z58 12:25 SunO Canton to Aberthaw as far as Barry, owing to engineering work. The train is approaching Barry Dock station.

**Right:** The line to Barry Docks is, depending on your point of view, a mere shadow of its former self, or a fascinating little line that sweeps through two 180-degree curves to get from the main line to its destination. Chemicals were the mainstay of traffic in the 1990s with No 1 dock receiving styrene from Baglan Bay in TEAs. The line around No 2 dock to the Dow Corning and BP chemical works received vinyl chloride monomer from Burn Naze in TDAs, silicon sand from France in IRBs and acrylonitrile from Immingham in Tiphook Rail TIAs.

Container traffic to the docks, again mostly for the chemical works, was introduced in December 1998, bringing into use the quayside lines again for the first time since grain traffic had finished in the 1980s. The daily train was a favourite chuck-out turn for one of South Wales's Class 37s, and on this occasion No 37402 *Bont Y Bermo* has six IRBs, one TIA and 12 fully laden FCAs in tow (albeit with empty containers), forming the 6B39 14:25 Barry Docks to ADJ train. The Dow Corning works is in the background and the train has only just started its journey, making its way past one of the frozen former timber ponds on Thursday 3 January 2002.

The Cardiff Bay to Cardiff Queen Street shuttle service effectively runs on an isolated piece of track between the two stations, not interfering or crossing any other service in the course of its travels. For this reason it was possible to introduce a 'non-standard' piece of kit to run the line, in the form of Pressed Steel Company's Class 121 unit No 121032.

The unit began service on 18 August 2006, but was quickly withdrawn the same day due to a fault and did not appear in regular service until the following month. The unit is cleared to run on other parts of the network but, because of crashworthiness standards, is not allowed to run in passenger service over them. The only time it has run outside its normal duties so far have been turning trips via the City Line, Radyr and Llandaff and crew-training runs to Abercynon, along the Vale of Glamorgan line to Bridgend or a one off trip to Lydney. On just such an occasion the 'bubble car' is seen between Cadoxton and Barry Dock stations with the 5Z30 09:53 Canton Sidings to Bridgend via Barry driver-training trip on Wednesday 18 April 2007. The line to Barry Docks heads downgrade on the left, past the relic of an old semaphore gantry.

While there are several track geometry and ultrasonic test trains in use around Britain, unique on the network is the Structure Gauging Train, which measures the distances of platforms, tunnels and various other structures in relation to the track. This means that each line can be assigned a specific loading gauge that might, for instance, restrict 9ft 6in containers being carried on anything other than well wagons. The bent chimney pots and scraped cylinder boxes on several steam engines bear witness to the fact that both the alignment and level of the track are constantly changing due to engineering work, so the importance of this gauging work cannot be underestimated.

In this case EWS No 37669 with RDB977470, RDB977468, DB975280, DC460000 (the optical structure gauging wagon) and DB975081 are forming a 1Z06 18:21 service, visiting Margam-Aberthaw-Cardiff (reverse)-Barry Island (reverse)-Penarth curve-Radyr (reverse)-Penarth curve-Aberthaw-Bridgend (reverse)-Pontyclun-Cardiff-Bristol Temple Meads (reverse)-Cardiff-Penarth (reverse)-Cardiff-Newport Godfrey Road (02:10). The train has paused at Barry station to wait for a unit to clear the line from Barry Island, allowing this unusual night shot to be obtained on Wednesday 27 March 2002.

Despite the attention that No 37402 received when it was outshopped in a revised two-tone Railfreight scheme with a darker upper band than normal, this wasn't in fact the first loco to have been painted in this livery. That honour fell to No 37675 *Margam TMD*, named after the depot whose dedicated staff carried out the work on both these magnificent engines. The first beasty to receive the livery is depicted here on Friday 28 December 2001 with ten loaded TEAs behind it, running as the 6B89 11:10 MFO 'Q' Tidal-Aberthaw PS service. The train is passing through Barry station, which until 31 October 2004 had a magnificent three-arm gantry semaphore at its south end, visible in this view.

The driver will be on his toes here as the 1 in 233/81/218/87 of Porthkerry bank is made even more difficult by the sharp 90-degree sweep away from Barry and the dampness of Porthkerry No 1 and No 2 tunnels. The sight and sound of this train as it crosses over Porthkerry Viaduct and through Porthkerry Park has been known to turn adults' heads, make enthusiasts bellow and cause young children to cry!

The line to Barry Island sweeps off to the right.

DRS's first appearance in South Wales was in the summer of 1998 when Class 20s and 37s in various eclectic combinations were hired in by Freightliner to work the 4S81 Pengam to Coatbridge service.

The only time DRS has appeared in its own right has been on route-learners and during December 2003, when an engineering blockade at Gloucester forced the Bridgwater flask train to run via the North & West route to Crewe. Their first ever revenue earning run to (rather than through) Wales was on Wednesday 14 October 2009, when 66423 hauled 7 KEAs and 8 JRAs of loaded scrap as the 6Z67 10:58 Shipley – Tidal. Subsequent trains have also run from Stockton and Tyne Dock. DRS's traction has also appeared as power for Victa Westlink 'Poshex's, 'Ruggex' specials, Stobart Rail charters and, as is this case, Serco-operated test trains.

No 37607, topped'n'tailed with classmate 37608, is in charge of the 1Z14 07:39 Swansea Maliphant to Derby RTC Track Inspection Train, running via the Vale of Glamorgan to Cardiff, back via the Vale again to Margam and thence to Derby via Pontyclun and Lydney. The location for this scene is Rhoose on the Vale of Glamorgan line, and the date is Friday 16 March 2007.

The vast majority of FGW services in South Wales are run between Swansea/Cardiff and Paddington. Having pulled out of providing the Fishguard Harbour trains, FGW services west of Swansea consist of just a daily train to and from Carmarthen and the twice-daily, Saturdays only, summer-dated services from Pembroke Dock.

The Great Western Trains and First Great Western franchises have gone through well over half a dozen livery changes since the contracts were first awarded in February 1996. The is the latest 'Neon' or 'Wavy Lines' version, as applied to Nos 43015 and 43092, running through Aberthaw with the diverted 12:30 Swansea to Paddington service on St David's Day 2009.

In the background is Aberthaw signal box and on the left the reception sidings for Aberthaw Power Station, with a rake of empty HTAs stabled.

**Above:** One of the most surprising events of 2008 was the resumption of revenue-earning rail traffic from Lafarge's Aberthaw Cement Works. It was thought to be well over 15 years since rail traffic had last been dispatched from here, which at that time used Presflo wagons.

The trains to Uskmouth replaced those from Westbury Cement Works, which was being mothballed at the time. The flow of cement was, when combined with the flow of concreting aggregate from Machen, being used in the construction of the new Combined Cycle Gas Turbine power station on the site of the previously demolished Uskmouth 'A' PS.

The rail loading facilities and track to the cement silo at Aberthaw had fallen into disrepair many years previously, so wagons were loaded in the former 'merry-go-round' (mgr) sidings by internal lorry. On the historic occasion of the first train, No 66512, with one empty and 13 loaded PCAs, sits in the works waiting the right away. The wagons had arrived the previous Monday evening and had been loaded over the course of the following three days. Thursday 27 November saw No 66512 arrive light engine from Bristol and depart as the 6Z36 21:15 Aberthaw to Uskmouth. The last loaded train ran on Monday 7 September 2009.

**Right:** Sunday 4 December 2005 was the day chosen to celebrate the end of Rhymney loco-hauled passenger services the following week. As we now know, this proved not to be the case, but certainly at the time everyone thought history was in the making. Locos from EWS, the West Coast Railway Company (WCRC), Project Defiance, and The Fifty Fund were used in various top'n'tail combinations, throughout a well-organised and thoroughly enjoyable day.

In this instance, WCRC's Nos 33207 and 47854 are seen entering Cardiff from Canton ready to form the 1Z40 12:56 SunO Cardiff to Rhymney. The River Taff in the foreground, the Millennium Stadium in the background and a magic combination of sun and storm clouds combined to produce the best shot of the day.

This day was notable for No 33207 as it was its first set of workings since being transferred from DRS to the WCRC. It was also its first working in WCRC colours and was also thought to be its first passenger working since being withdrawn by EWS!

**Left:** Following the closure of the coking-coal-producing collieries in the east of Wales, British Steel relied on imports through the deep-water harbour at Port Talbot to satisfy its needs. Up to five trains a day were run between Port Talbot and Llanwern in order to meet the latter's requirements for producing coke to smelt the iron ore.

Over the years Class 37/7s gave way to 56s, which in turn gave way to Class 66s, and the length of train was increased in stages from 30 to 35 to 40 wagons. In the last stage of evolution of this train, No 66045 and 40 HCA/HFAs are seen with the 6B50 09:00 Port Talbot Grange to Llanwern Coal Siding, coasting through the inappropriately named (for a Welsh location) St Georges on Friday 29 December 2000.

**Above:** For a long time now, Port Talbot Steelworks has had the ability to produce more steel than it can roll. Llanwern, on the other hand, has had more rolling capacity than the steel it could produce.

Thus for many years, as well as iron ore and coal, there was a steady flow of slab between the two plants to cater for this imbalance.

As both Port Talbot and Llanwern were considered to be effectively one works, either plant could supply its customers' needs, depending on which was most suitable at the time. This and the inter-works traffic could lead to the false impression that various products were being sent to destinations that could not actually handle such traffic, as is the case here, where No 60006 *Scunthorpe Ironmaster* in British Steel Blue livery is captured hauling 16 BAA/BFA/BBAs of slab as the 6B71 10:20 SunO Margam to Ebbw Vale via Llanwern.

Although it would seem that the slab was destined for Ebbw Vale, all of these wagons will in fact be dropped at Llanwern and a set of different coil wagons picked up there for Ebbw Vale. The location is St Georges on Sunday 23 January 2000.

### Bridgend and Port Talbot area: main line, valleys and branches

As part of its planning consent, all the coal produced from the Margam opencast site had to leave by rail instead of road, using the adjacent dedicated Parc Slip loading point. The first train ran on 6 August 1996 and since then Class 37s, 56s, 60s and 66s have taken coal in FCAs, FPAs, HAAs, HCAs, HDAs, HFAs, HMAs, JRAs and MEAs to four cement works (Westbury, Plymstock, Hope and Rugby), three power stations (Didcot, Ironbridge and Fifoots), two steelworks (Llanwern and Port Talbot) and three locations for blending (Onllwyn, Cwmbargoed and Newport Docks).

Coal from the Upper 9-foot seam was ideal for making into coke, and as such provided the only domestic Welsh coal to Port Talbot steelworks since the early 1990s. The coal was first conveyed in 30-foot Russell containers mounted on eight twin FCA wagons, then later in JRA bogie box wagons, 12 of which are seen here at Parc Slip behind No 66077 *Benjamin Gimbert G.C.* on Friday 19 September 2009. After loading, the train will depart as the 6F78 18:00 to Port Talbot Grange.

The last train from Parc Slip ran (to Onllwyn) on Saturday 7 March 2009. However, at the time of writing the result of an inquiry into an extension is awaited with interest.

After BP Amoco closed the last remaining part of its works at Baglan Bay on 31 March 2004, a number of trains were run to clear the area of contaminated spoil. Freightliner Heavy Haul won the contract and the first train ran from Baglan Bay to Calvert on 11 June 2004. Just over seven weeks later, the destination was switched to Appleford, and four weeks after that the last train to here ran on 24 August.

The loaded trains ran at night, but the inbound empties provided the ideal opportunity for an evening shot. Here No 66601 *The Hope Valley* has 24 MJAs for company as the 6Z43 12:55 Calvert to Baglan Bay, approaching Margam Moors Junction on Friday 25 June 2004. As paths over the single-track Claydon to Oxford route are at a premium, this train had to run to its booked path or be delayed, which then had a knock-on effect for loading at Baglan. This led to the interesting sight of the first two wagons still being loaded, presumably as there was not enough time for them to be unloaded at Calvert before the train had to leave.

In April 1998 EWS named and painted one of its Class 37s, No 37428, as the dedicated loco for the prestigious 'Royal Scotsman' train, which operates in Scotland during the summer season. In 2000 No 37428's reliability problems led to a spell in the works and, in the middle of the 'Royal Scotsman' season, found itself in South Wales.

The MBA 'Monster Box' wagons were built at Thrall Europa's York works in 1999 as part of an EWS order for 2,500 new wagons. Unfortunately, they didn't seem to find as much use as intended, and as early as July 2000 two sets of wagons were taken from Llanwern and Margam to Wakefield to be converted to low-height MCA outer and MDA inner wagons at Horbury.

Both moves utilised No 37428 *Royal Scotsman*. The Llanwern train ran to York on Tuesday 4 July 2000. This was followed on Friday 7 July by the 11 MBAs on this train, the 6Z42 15:00 Margam to Wakefield, pictured leaving Margam Moors.

One has to love the irony of a loco supposedly dedicated to Scotland, hauling a luxury train around beautiful scenery, instead actually in the depths of South Wales, hauling a bunch of dirty wagons amidst heavy industrial landscapes!

The introduction of the creeping 'red death' in 1998, combined with Keith Heller's 'Sweating the Assets' policy in 2004, led to the total elimination of EWS's Class 20s, 31s, 33s, 47s, 56s, 58s and 73s, as well as a serious reduction in the ranks of the company's 37s and 60s.

These mass withdrawals led to line-ups such as this one, which, when seen in September 2007, consisted of 19 locos, in three classes, five sub-classes and ten different liveries. Nos 56062, 37413, 37428, 56100, 37896, 37698, 37890, 37692, 37684, 37798, 37675, 37415, 37412, 37898, 37704, 37670, 37669, 47761 and 47772 sit quietly rusting away, awaiting their fates with the preservation movement, a train operator, or the scrapman.

The following 2¼ years saw the line-up much reduced as Nos 37403 (out of sight to the left) and 37413 went for preservation at the Bo'ness & Kinneil Railway; No 37412 went to Barrow Hill for reinstatement by DRS; Nos 37669 and 37670 went to Toton and Knottingley respectively for later reinstatement by EWS; Harry Needle's No 37704 went to the scrapman at Stockton while his other loco, 37898, went to store at Long Marston; No 47761 went to Butterley for the '47401 Project' and No 47772 went to Carnforth for use by the West Coast Railway Company. In February 2010, out of the above list, only No 37675 and the 2 class 56's remained at Margam; the remaining eight class 37s all having been disposed of, initially at least, for scrap.

**Left:** Class 20s were always rare visitors to South Wales. Their only 'regular' duties here saw them appear on the Hunslet Barclay weedkilling trains until this train finished in 1998. Under DRS, the 'Choppers' have appeared on freightliner trains from Pengam and route-learners between Crewe and Cardiff for a Knowsley to Wentloog train, which unfortunately never started. They appeared again over the Heart of Wales line on behalf of a future Stobart Pullman railtour, which unfortunately never came off either!

Cotswold Rail has hired Harry Needle Railroad Company's (HNRCs) Nos 20901 and 20905 for several duties over the years, two of which saw them enter South Wales. The first was on Friday 8 February 2008 when the pair came to Margam to collect HNRCs No 37704 and take it Bristol Temple Meads. The second time was on Wednesday 13 February 2008 when the same two 20s, barrier coach 6330 and No 47375, came to collect No 37898 and take it to Long Marston. The sight and sound of a pair of 20s shunting Margam engineer's sidings in 2008 was most unusual and highly evocative. With Margam depot in the background, the latter of the two trains is seen leaving Margam's engineer's/storage sidings as the 5Z80 16:30 to Horton Road.

**Right:** Heol Y Deliaid pedestrian crossing at the north end of Margam Yard gives unique views of shunting and industrial operations centred on Port Talbot Steelworks. From this footpath No 08995 *Kidwelly* is seen engaged in shunting a BYA, two JSAs and a KIA on Monday 17 January 2000.

Never has the term 'revolutionary' been more appropriately applied in rail terms than to the High Speed Trains. However, after nearly 30 years of being mercilessly thrashed from pillar to post, the Paxman Valenta RP200L engines were becoming life-expired. As the HST2 programme had been shelved, the decision was made to give the FGW HST fleet a mid-life overhaul, which involved replacing the Paxman engines with quieter and more fuel-efficient MTU 16V 4000 units instead. The engine replacements were carried out at Brush Works in Loughborough while the electrical equipment was refurbished or replaced at Landore in Swansea.

The contract to take Valenta-fitted HSTs to Brush and bring MTU-fitted HSTs back to Landore/St Phillips Marsh/Laira was awarded to Cotswold Rail, and it commenced these moves in January 2006, taking over from Freightliner. Thus, on the pleasant evening of Monday 21 August 2006 No 47828 *Joe Strummer* with No 43141, buffet 10235 and No 47813 *John Peel* are seen passing Margam with the 5Z83 18:35 Landore to Laira. At Laira, the locos would pick up No 43164 and return to Gloucester, continuing to Brush the next day.

With some blooming flora adding a splash of colour to the picture, No 60031 *Ben Lui* is seen coasting through Port Talbot with a set of 34 HAA/HDA and HMAs in tow, loaded with more than 1,000 tonnes of Wales's finest black stuff. The date is Monday 22 May 2000 and at the time the Onllwyn trains were easy to identify as they consisted of 34 mgr wagons compared to the 36 run everywhere else, the length of train being limited by the run-round loop at Onllwyn.

Changes to the layout at Onllwyn in 2005 enabled the train of 17 HTAs (as was common by then) to be increased to 20, the same as the Avonmouth services. Following trials, this was increased to

21 HTAs in 2007, giving further efficiencies and an easy way to identify the train again! Nowadays, however, all power station trains are 21 HTAs in length.

By the time this book is published, work should just be about to start on stage two of the Port Talbot Peripheral Distributor Road. The bridge in this view, which is the main road access into the steelworks, will be replaced by the 'tunnel'-type Cefn Gwrgan bridge, which will carry the new dual carriageway on a skew over the main line.

**Left:** Iron ore, coal as coke, lime, scrap and a few other lesser ingredients are required to make steel in the Basic Oxygen process used by Tata in Britain. The iron ore for Port Talbot and Llanwern has, since 1974, come in through the deep-water harbour at Port Talbot. Conveyers from the harbour served Port Talbot's needs, while up to five trains a day ran between here and Llanwern. Over the years, trains have seen triple-headed Class 37s, pairs of heavyweight 37s, pairs of 56s and single Class 59/0s, 59/1s, 59/2s or 60s. When the trains were increased from 27 to 30 wagons from 4 March 1976, they became the heaviest trains on the BR network, until superseded by the Mendip stone trains.

The last train of iron ore ran in South Wales on Saturday 26 May 2001 and steelmaking finished at Llanwern on 26 June. Here No 59203 *Vale of Pickering*, a JTA, 28 JUAs and another JTA are seen forming the 7B40 07:54 Port Talbot Docks to Llanwern Tippler Siding on Wednesday 9 June 1999. The train is rumbling down the Port Talbot Harbour branch over some of the internal works lines. Port Talbot's Nos 4 and 5 blast furnaces dominate the background.

**Right:** Steelmaking in Port Talbot can be traced as far back as 1901, when Messrs Gilbertson of Pontardawe started building its steelworks adjacent to the north side of the docks. Baldwins Margam steelworks opened on the south side of the docks in 1918, followed by the Steel Company of Wales's Abbey Works in 1951. The first two works have closed, leaving just Tata's Port Talbot Works in production.

In 2008 Port Talbot's inward rail traffic included dolomite from Thrislington, scrap from Swindon and Laisterdyke, and slab from both Lackenby and abroad, imported via Newport Docks. Outgoing rail-hauled products saw slab going to Llanwern and coil to Corby, Hartlepool, Liverpool Gladstone Dock, Llanwern, Middlesbrough, Round Oak, Shotton, Trostre, Wolverhampton and various places abroad.

For internal shunting, the works employs a number of Brush Bo-Bo locomotives, fitted with either Rolls Royce DV8TCE or Perkins 3000 series CV12 engines. There are also a small number of 0-4-0 diesel shunters with Rolls Royce DV8 engines.

Having brought torpedo wagons Nos 11 (485 tons gross, 270 tare) and 20 (520 tons gross, 300 tare) up from No 5 blast furnace, No 906 is pushing them towards the BOS (Basic Oxygen Steel) plant, for final conversion into steel, on the pleasant evening of Sunday 18 July 1999.

**Left:** The first Class 67 duty in South Wales, and indeed the UK, occurred on Thursday 2 March 2000, when No 67004 worked the previous day's 1V44 23:20 Willesden Princess Royal Distribution Centre (PRDC) to Swansea Travelling Post Office (TPO) forward from Bristol Temple Meads. The loco was meant to have worked the previous day's inbound 1M95 21:40 Swansea to Willesden TPO as far as Bristol, but a microprocessor fault prevented that and the train had to be topped by No 47738, thus in fact becoming the first Class 67 failure in revenue-earning service!

The 30 Class 67s were meant to replace almost twice that number of 47s on Res and TPO duties, as well as being available for railtours and charters over the weekend. The complete collapse of mail by rail is well documented and although the Class 67s are, in 2009, once again fully utilised, it certainly is not for the duties for which they were originally intended.

Here, the last member of the class, No 67030, has a four-car PCV (Propelling Control Vehicle) set behind it as the 1M06 14:25 Swansea to Willesden PRDC, approaching Port Talbot Parkway station on Monday 21 August 2000. This service was withdrawn from Friday 9 January 2004 and the last mail train ever to run in Wales arrived in the early hours of Saturday 21 February 2004, when No 67008 and a four-PCV set worked Friday's 1V34 20:30 Willesden PRDC to Swansea, bringing the end of an era.

**Above:** Pressure tanks by rail, of any type, are distinguished by having a horizontal orange band along the centre of the wagon. In Wales these wagons have been used to carry, among other things, Liquid Petroleum Gas (LPG) from Fawley to Monds at Clydach on Tawe; oxygen from Ditton to Margam; Vinyl Chloride Monomer (VCM) from Burn Naze to Barry; and propylene from Partington and later Humber to Baglan Bay. The returning empties of this latter service are seen here behind No 56067, which has 12 TDA and three TCAs behind it as the 6E21 08:20 TFO Baglan Bay to Humber on Tuesday 6 July 1999. The train is approaching Port Talbot, and its origin can be seen on the horizon in the distance.

Freightliner took over the running of this train from 3 March 2002, until, following the closure of Baglan's isopropanol facility, it finished in early 2004. Thus the train provided the first regular work for FHH in South Wales, as well as the last opportunity to see pressure tanks of any variety, anywhere in the principality.

**Left:** When the South Wales & West franchise became Wales & West in December 1997, the TOC decided on a new livery for its fleet. No 158867 was repainted in an unusual purple, blue and silver livery for evaluation purposes. Presumably the trial was not a success, as no other units were repainted. Thus in this entirely unique colour scheme, No 158867 is captured slowing for its stop at Baglan on Tuesday 2 May 2000 with the 15:16 Pembroke Dock to Manchester Piccadilly service.

**Above:** MoD traffic in West Wales saw a downturn in the late 1980s and early '90s following the closure of the Royal Naval Armament Depots (RNAD) at both Newton Noyes in 1989 and Trecwn in 1991. However, in the late 1990s MoD traffic could still be seen in the form of vehicles, armoured personnel carriers and tanks being transported to the Castlemartin firing ranges south of Pembroke

from the likes of Ludgershall, Warminster and Redmire. The most convenient offloading location at Pembroke Dock is unfortunately limited to all but the smallest of vehicles because of the restrictive clearances in Pembroke Tunnel. As a result, most vehicles are loaded and offloaded at Haverfordwest on the Milford Haven branch.

Returning after exercises, Nos 47298/D1100 *Pegasus* in the original 'Speedlink' livery and 47216 *Arnold Kunzler* in Railfreight Distribution livery are seen here with seven KFAs, 18 KWA/KWBs and a single VAA van for company, loaded with armoured personnel carriers, forming the 6X43 14:40 Haverfordwest–Ludgershall. It is Saturday 18 April 1998 and the train is roaring through the well-known and picturesque location of Briton Ferry.

**Right:** In the late 1990s there were two TPO trains in South Wales, one between Cardiff and Shieldmuir (with the set being based at Bristol), and one between Swansea and Willesden PRDC (with the set being based at Margam).

The ECS to form the Swansea train ran as the 5M95 18:37 from Margam and is seen here on Tuesday 7 September 1999 behind an unidentified Class 47 crossing the 389-yard Landore Viaduct. Upon arrival at Swansea, the PCV on the back of the train will be used to reverse the formation into Maliphant sidings, where the 47 will run round and propel the whole lot back into Platform 1, ready to form that night's 1M95 21:40 to Willesden.

The last TPO train to depart from Wales was the 1M95 service, which left Swansea behind No 67008 on Friday 25 July 2003. The last TPO to arrive was in the early hours of the next morning, when No 67018 worked in on Friday's 1V44 23:20 from Willesden PRDC, before returning ECS to Margam.

In the mid 1990s, BP's Baglan Bay chemical works received by rail acetic acid (more commonly known as vinegar) from Saltend at Hull and propylene from Humber. In return it dispatched ethanol to Hull and styrene to Barry No 1 dock as well as later to Stalybridge.

In the distance, yellow works shunter ZZ267 is already on its way to the discharge point with the 16 TTAs of acetic acid that No 66115 had just dropped off via the 6V14 07:30 MWFO from Hull Saltend. After discharge the wagons will be taken further into the plant, cleaned and reloaded with ethanol in readiness for the

backload to Hull. Therefore this view of the exchange sidings on Monday 5 June 2000 shows No 66115 and 15 TTAs of ethanol about to form the 6E33 20:15 MWFO departure to Saltend.

Both the vinyl acetate monomer plant and the ethanol plant at Baglan Bay were closed in December 2001, being replaced by a new vinyl acetate plant at Hull. This resulted in the end of both the acetic acid and ethanol flows, and the last inward train of vinegar tanks ran on 18 January 2002.

**Above:** Of the two operational Class 50s on the main line in 2006, No 50049 belonged to 'Project Defiance' and 50031 to 'The Fifty Fund', which also operated non-main-line-certified Nos D444 and 50035 on the Severn Valley Railway. The two groups always had close ties and this was confirmed on 1 January 2007 when the 'Class 50 Alliance' was officially formed, bringing all four machines under one umbrella.

In 2006 ATW signed a three-year agreement with the groups to provide power for various trains and this famously led to their use on the summer-dated Fishguard Harbour services. The normal routing of the 1B96 10:55 Cardiff to Fishguard Harbour was via Pontyclun and the Swansea District Line. However, for the final week of the summer 2006 timetable the train was diverted to run each way via the Landore loop instead. Thus No 50049 *Defiance* is seen with the 1B97 13:35 EWD Fishguard Harbour to Cardiff Central, crossing Loughor Viaduct on Friday 8 September 2006, the penultimate run of this train.

Changes are due here in the future as the viaduct will eventually be replaced by a new structure and the single track doubled in order to improve reliability, increase capacity and allow new stations to be built. This should also eventually allow the Swansea District Line to be singled.

**Right:** Under privatisation, the Central Services locos responsible for providing power for the various track-testing trains fell into EWS ownership. EWS soon dispensed with these Class 20s and 47/9s, preferring instead to use its fleet of Res 47s. Therefore No 47781 *Isle of Iona* is seen top'n'tailing classmate No 47749 *Atlantic College* with the Track Inspection Train, as the 1Z12 08:50 Carmarthen to Swansea. The working appears to be a simple one, but as with most Serco workings it belies the fact that the train will travel via Pembroke Dock, the Swansea District Line, all three sides of the Jersey Marine triangle, Swansea Burrows, Onllwyn, Cwmgwrach and Cockett to reach its destination! Space does not allow a full description of this train's tortuous itinerary, but suffice to say that the crew had to change ends 14 times on its 10-hour journey. The train is crossing the magnificent 150-yard Neath River swing-bridge on Thursday 14 August 2003.

**Left:** The siding at Steel Supply was used as a coal-blending site in the early 1990s. Once blending began at Aberthaw PS itself in March 1996, the site was renamed Jersey Marine and was used as a stone-loading area for RMC (Ready Mixed Concrete), which, from April 1998 onwards, began sending trains to Leeds and Ely.

In April 1999 the terminal was taken over by Aggregate Industries (AI) and EWS was contracted to take gritstone to such destinations as Thorney Mill, Brentford and Angerstein Wharf. AI was bought out by Holcim in 2005 and Freightliner took over the running of the Holcim contract from 1 April 2006, renaming the Jersey Marine terminal again, this time to Neath AWF.

When Holcim (which is still trading as AI) bought out Foster Yeoman in 2006, the terminal, as well as serving its original destinations of Thorney Mill and Angerstein Wharf, also began to serve new places such as Harlow Mill, Theale, Crawley, Burngullow, Tavistock Junction and Croft.

However, back in EWS days, No 66051 is seen in the terminal with a rake of HGAs and Caib PGAs on Friday 5 May 2000. Once loaded, the train will form a 6Z97 13:10 to Westbury via a run-round at Swansea Burrows, before going forward later the same evening for unloading at Thorney Mill.

**Above:** No 09101 *Ivor* has two IVAs in tow as it trundles slowly down the branch from Ford's Visteon plant to Swansea Burrows on Tuesday 30 March 2004. The vans had arrived earlier in the day at Burrows from Dagenham by way of Bridgend and will return the same way that evening.

The trip from Bridgend to Swansea, and return, was undertaken via the Vale of Glamorgan, Penarth Curve, Leckwith Loop and Bridgend. Unfortunately it was deemed uneconomic for such a short load and the traffic finished running by rail in December 2004, subsequently being roaded instead.

The magnificent building behind the shunter is the former Dan-y-Graig steam shed, then in use by Gower Chemicals, which had in previous years also sent traffic out by rail.

**Left:** In the early 'noughties' Swansea Docks was busy with container traffic, import and export coal, import and export slab, import and export steel coil, export wire coil and export tinplate, although obviously not all at the same time!

In this photograph No 08994 *Gwendraeth* has eight empty BDAs, BFAs and BMAs in tow, leaving No 3 quay in Swansea Docks. The slab that had been transported on these wagons had come from Port Talbot Steelworks and was destined for export to Ymuiden in the Netherlands. The date of this photograph is Friday 29 September 2000, before Llanwern's blast furnaces shut in June 2001, after which slab has been imported rather than exported.

**Above:** The washery and disposal point at Onllwyn was once served by its own drift mines and surrounding collieries. However, in July 2009 it takes in coal from three opencast sites at Selar, Nant Helen and the East Pit East Revised scheme. At Onllwyn the coal is washed, graded, blended and sorted according to its customers' demands.

In this instance No 60083 has 18 PFAs for company loaded with former Cawood containers. The train is seen departing from Onllwyn some 90 minutes early as the 7B79 20:51 to Swansea Burrows on Thursday 21 May 1998. The containers are eventually destined for Cardiff Docks for export to Ireland.

**Above:** The line to Aberpergwm Colliery closed in 1985 and with it went the line down the Vale of Neath to Neath & Brecon Junction. However, following a railtour in October 1993 the line reopened in March 1994, but to a new loading pad built by Ryan Mining as part of the redevelopment of Pentreclwydau Nos 1 and 2 south drifts.

The history of the area since that time is far too complicated to be written here, but suffice to say that after Ryan went bust, the coal traffic loaded at Cwmgwrach in later years actually came mostly from Energybuild's Aberpergwm mine and Nant Y Mynydd opencast site across the valley from Pentreclwydau. With that company's coal in tow, No 66117 is seen with 19 HTAs rumbling down the Cwmgwrach branch at Tonna, with the 6C32 13:08 WFO (13:10 SO) Cwmgwrach to Aberthaw on Wednesday 1 November 2006.

However, from May 2007 Energybuild's coal was loaded onto rail at the Tower pad instead, meaning that the Vale of Neath line once again fell into disuse. However, Unity had previously taken over the development of the Pentreclwydau mine and was due to begin coaling in 2010. If the much-talked-about production targets are met (if!), there could be up to three trains a day from here in the future, instead of the previous three trains a week!

**Right:** As well as coal, Cwmgwrach has seen use as a stone-loading point both for Aggregate Industries (before it moved to Neath AWF in April 1999) and for F. Parnell's Bwlch Ffos quarry. No 60083 is seen with 17 Bardon PHAs being filled with gritstone from AI's Cwm Nant Leici quarry. It is Friday 22 May 1998 and, after completion of loading, the train will depart for Hither Green, going forward the next day to Thorney Mill.

**Left:** In 1984 BREL and Metro-Cammell each built two prototype 'Sprinters' (Nos 150001/002 and 151001/002 respectively) for evaluation purposes, as a prelude to a new build of second-generation Diesel Multiple Unit's (DMU's). Following exhaustive testing, it was BREL that won the contract and, starting in 1985, built 50 Class 150/1s and 85 Class 150/2s for passenger use.

In addition, BREL constructed a heavily modified 51st Class 150/1 unit for BR's Railway Technical Centre. The set is numbered No 950001 (formed of cars 999600 and 999601) and is known as the Track Recording Unit, or TRU for short. It carries out the same functions as the Track Inspection Train (no acronym allowed!) but tends to visit the lesser-known branch lines and rural backwaters where there are route availability issues.

No such issues here, but the Heart of Wales line could certainly be regarded as one of Britain's lesser-used routes, which is perhaps why, on Wednesday 8 February 2006, No 950001 is seen trundling over the Afon Sawdde river bridge working the 2Z08 07:20 Shrewsbury to Shrewsbury via the Heart of Wales line, reversing at Morlais Junction.

**Above:** There is just one set of independent snowploughs in South Wales, based at Margam, and they are tested once a year prior to the snowy season.

The 2Z99 09:00 Margam TC to Margam TC via Llanelli and the Swansea District Line is formed of snowplough ZZA ADB965235, Nos 66154 and 66063, and snowplough ZZA ADB965223. The date is Sunday 21 January 2007 and the train is passing Llangennech. The drivers of these trains really do have to have good route knowledge since, as can be seen, vision is severely impaired.

**Above:** Rail Management Services (RMS) Locotec has the contract with Corus's Packaging Plus tinplating works at Trostre to provide all its rail requirements (shunters, staff, servicing, etc), replacing the former incumbent, Hunslet Barclay.

RMS Locotec was originally solely a provider of shunting locomotives to a variety of companies, being part of the Ealing Community Trust (ECT) group of companies. However, when ECT's 'Mainline Rail' company was wound up in early 2008, its fleet of Class 31s was transferred to RMS Locotec. Shortly after, in September 2008, ECT sold its rail assets to Iowa Pacific Holdings, which, under its British American Railway Services (BARS) Ltd arm, now runs the Trostre contract.

Thus No H015 *SYLGWYN* is seen bringing six BCAs and BLAs out of the Pickling Line bay to be taken back to Port Talbot for reloading on Monday 27 October 2008. Out of sight to the left is No H028, the former 08622, which acts as a standby in case of failure. At peak production, two trains a day, every day, are booked to serve Trostre, bringing hot rolled coil in and taking tinplate out. In 2008 tinplate by rail from Trostre, the last remaining rail-connected tinplate works in the country, was going to Worcester, Carlisle, France and Germany.

## Main line and branches west of Swansea

One of my favourite little spots for photographing is along the Millennium Coastal Park to the west of Llanelli. This Welsh version of Dawlish has a number of opportunities all the year round. In the winter it provides one of the very few locations in Wales where silhouette shots can be achieved, the abundance of mountainous terrain proving to make life rather difficult in other locations!

On Thursday 24 January 2008 an unidentified Class 175/0 runs through Pwll with the 15:10 Milford Haven to Manchester Piccadilly service as the dying embers of the setting sun cast their deep red shadows over the golden ponds and willowy reeds of … blah blah blah etc etc etc!

The VSOE is a sumptuous train that travels mainly in the south of Britain to offer passengers the luxury of train travel from a bygone age. Such is the popularity of these trips that an equally opulent sister train was introduced on 31 May 2000, known as the 'Northern Belle'.

On Monday 12 December 2005 the 'Northern Belle' ran a Christmas Lunch trip from Bristol Temple Meads and Cardiff to Carmarthen and back. Not even deluxe trains are without their problems, and the original loco, No 67030, failed at Bristol with a fire bell fault before the tour started. No 66155 was pinched off the 6C01 Bristol East Depot steel trip and topped the train to Margam with the 67 tucked inside to provide train heat. At Margam the pair were swapped for No 67021, which then worked the remainder of the trip. Under the setting sun and rising moon, the 1Z53 11:54 from Bristol is seen alongside Cefn Padrig Bay, west of Llanelli, running 72 minutes late.

Like a muppet, I somehow managed to take this shot using Tungsten film, so the nice folk at Ian Allan have colour-corrected it for me!

In 2001 a new 19.3km-long, 600mm-diameter gas pipeline was to be built between Pontyates and Banc-y-Felin for Transco. Therefore between 9 and 23 April 2001 nine trains were run from Hartlepool to Margam and then Margam to Llandeilo Junction Yard, where the lengthy train was split into two portions to enable it to fit into the stockyard at Carmarthen sidings.

The third train in the sequence arrived at Llandeilo Junction on Wednesday 11 April 2001, having departed from Hartlepool the night before. Unfortunately, the foot and mouth epidemic prevented access to the more scenic locations, so, with the first portion having already been unloaded earlier that morning, this photograph shows the second portion, the 6G76 10:36 Llandeilo Junction to Carmarthen, reversing into the sidings at Carmarthen. No 66138 was the chosen power for 11 BDAs and BEAs of pipes, seen here after having run round in the station in the background. After unloading, the empties will return as the 6Z47 17:01 Carmarthen to Hartlepool, picking up the first set of empties at Llandeilo Junction on its way through.

For obvious reasons the movements of the Royal Train are made under conditions of strict secrecy and are not even entered onto the TOPS/TRUST/GEMINI systems. However, some details of the Royal Family's engagements are available on its website and if the method of travel is not specified, one can always take pot luck as to how the member will be arriving, and go out on the off chance!

On Tuesday 12 July 2005 Nos 67005 *Queen's Messenger* and 67006 *Royal Sovereign* have eight of the Royal coaches between them after arriving in Carmarthen with the initial stop of the first annual tour of Wales by the Prince of Wales and Duchess of Cornwall. After being greeted at the station, the Royal couple then visited the Gelli Aur Agricultural College near Llandeilo to see how the Prince's Trust Cymru was helping young people start in agriculture. The train meanwhile returned ECS to and from Margam, before taking the Prince of Wales to Cardiff for a dining trip with invited guests to Llanelli and back.

The Carmarthen & Cardigan (C&C) Railway opened between Carmarthen Town and Conwil on 3 September 1860, being extended to Llandyssul in 1864 and as far as Newcastle Emlyn (vice Cardigan) by the GWR in 1895. BR passenger services ended in stages in the 1950s and '60s, but it took until 30 September 1973 before the final death of goods in the area.

The former C&C is home to two of South Wales's preservation lines. The Gwili Railway was the first standard-gauge preservation line in Wales, running its inaugural train in 1978. A bit further down the line is the narrow gauge Teifi Valley Railway (TVR), which ran its first train on 24 August 1985.

In this view, taken on Sunday 20 September 2009, *Sgt Murphy* heads four home-built coaches away from the new station at Henllan towards Llandyfriog (Riverside) as the 14:30 departure. The original TVR station was behind the camera. This 'extension' was opened on the site of the original C&C station in July 2009. In the background can be seen the shed and a few standard-gauge shunters. *Sgt Murphy* was once resident at the Penrhyn Slate Quarries and was named after the quarry-owner's horse that won the Grand National in both 1921 and 1923.

The Class 155 'Sprinters' were built by British Leyland at Workington and were introduced to BR's Provincial sector from 1987. However, in 1991 and 1992, shortly after the introduction of the Class 158s, 35 of the 42 units were split, modified and formed into 70 Class 153s at Hunslet-Barclay in Kilmarnock. They are ideal for lightly loaded services such as the one depicted here, the 11:05 Pembroke Dock to Swansea, pictured bumping along the jointed track at Manorbier Newton on the Pembroke Dock branch, with No 153320 in charge. The date is Saturday 16 September 2006 and, although Class 153s are sufficient for traffic levels on this line in the winter months, WAG subsidies allow two-car Class 150/2s to be provided during the summer, and the number of passengers even justifies FGW running summer-dated HSTs.

As the oil trains to West Wales run almost exclusively overnight, pictures of them in the area are rather hard to come by. Thus on Saturday 22 July 2000, when it became known that a 6B25 10:48 SO Westerleigh to Robeston was running right the way through, all other matters were dropped and the long journey west began. The ideal location for the time of day proved to be just west of Whitland, where No 60098 *Charles Francis Brush*, the 1000th loco built by Brush, is seen sweeping round the curve away from the station making light work of its 23 TDAs and TEAs. The former Whitland creamery in the distance has since been demolished.

Freight in general is rather sparse in West Wales. The closure of the Herbrandston oil refinery in 1983, Newton Noyes RNAD in 1989, Trecwn RNAD in 1991 and the Waterston refinery in December 1997 was followed by the Hydro-Agri fertiliser depot at Carmarthen in 2001.

Other traffic has included fertiliser to Haverfordwest and pipes to Carmarthen (both 2001), as well as an 18-month flow of stone to Waterston, starting in April 2005, for the construction of new Liquid Natural Gas (LNG) tanks. The only 'regular' traffic over the years has been military trains to Haverfordwest or Pembroke Dock, but even these have only run as required.

Despite the resurgence of interest following the running of the summer-dated loco-hauled trains to Fishguard Harbour, the lines west of Llanelli are rarely photographed owing to the general lack of daytime freight and the preponderance of units. This is a shame as there are some genuinely nice locations to be found hidden away on the back roads around the area.

At Gelli on Saturday 7 April 2007 an unidentified Class 158 is seen heading west with the 14:00 Swansea to Milford Haven service. Most Milford Haven trains at the time were through services from Manchester Piccadilly, but on this occasion engineering work between Swansea and Cardiff in connection with the Port Talbot resignalling scheme necessitated the use of 'local' service trains instead.

The Serco track-testing trains in West Wales have generally operated three or four times a year and have seen a considerable variety of traction over the past 7 years. When I first started chasing them in 2003 it was Res Class 47s, followed by EWS 37s from February 2004 and EWS 66s intermixed with hired-in FMR 47s from February 2005. DRS Class 37s appeared from September 2006, until replaced by the Class 150 unit from June 2007. A further variation appeared on 18 June 2008 when Mainline Rail's No 31454 and Rail Vehicle Engineering Limited's (RVEL's) No 31190 operated a Track Inspection Coach because the Track Recording Unit was undergoing maintenance.

Back in 2005 EWS was still providing the traction and crews for these trains, but because it was short of traction at the time it was an extremely unusual but nevertheless highly pleasant surprise to find that Nos 47709 *Dionysos* and 47355 *Avocet* (in the revised Fragonset livery) had been hired in for the jaunt around West Wales.

Therefore on Wednesday 9 November 2005 the 1Z14 07:50 Swansea to Swansea via Pembroke Dock, Milford Haven and Fishguard Harbour is seen near Clunderwen in glorious winter lighting conditions. In these days of privatisation it is to be noted that the Serco-operated train was being run for Network Rail using FMR traction and crewed by EWS drivers!

In 2006 a fleet of new 102-tonne bogie tanks were built by VTG for Murco's oil traffic from its Robeston refinery. Most of the new wagons were delivered to Margam by wagonload services and tripped down on empty oil trains.

However, there was just one bulk delivery, when a set of 15 TEA wagons were delivered by FMR's No 47703 *Hermes* on Monday 24 July 2006. The 6Z59 11:00 Wembley to Robeston is seen running through Haverfordwest at speed. Rather outrageously, a pair of FMR Class 31s had been booked to do this move the week before, but because of a heatwave at the time (Wednesday 19 July was apparently the hottest day on record since 1911), multiple speed restrictions were being enforced countrywide and the backlog of trains meant that the service, although ready to go, was eventually caped. The fine former goods shed still stands in the background.

When first introduced in 1999, Railtrack's Multi Purpose Vehicles (MPVs) were cleverly designed to undertake Sandite duties in the autumn, de-icing duties in the winter and weedkilling duties in the spring, leaving the summer period for maintenance.

In South Wales, the autumn leaf-fall duties are undertaken by loco-hauled trains, and there are no de-icing duties in the winter, therefore the only time the MPVs can be seen is during the spring weedkilling season.

In this case, MPV Nos DR 98912/DR 98962 is seen on a tour around West Wales, working the 6Z10 13:30 Whitland to Whitland via Fishguard Harbour and Swansea on Monday 20 April 2009. The train has just come off the Fishguard branch and is heading for Swansea via Cockett. Clarbeston Road station is in the background.

The withdrawal of FGW from providing the daytime service to Fishguard Harbour from 31 August 2002 meant that, under the franchise rules, responsibility for providing this service fell to Wales & Borders.

The Rhymney loco-hauled trains remained at Cardiff Canton during the daytime, so, during the summer peak demand, it made sense to use these underutilised resources on an out-and-back service to West Wales in between their rush-hour duties. The first summer-dated trains began running in 2002 and continued each year until 2004. In 2005 the summer service ran with units; however, for one week during December a loco-hauled Fishguard train ran again, which ultimately proved to be the last fling for Class·37s on these trains. The last set of loco-hauled trains to Fishguard ran in the summer of 2006 using Class 50s.

On Bank Holiday Monday, 25 August 2003, No 37422 *Cardiff Canton TMD* has paused at Clarbeston Road signal box to hand over the token while working the 1R38 13:35 EWD Fishguard Harbour to Rhymney. The line to Milford Haven, Robeston and Waterston, as well as the former branches to Neyland and Herbrandston, curves off to the left.